THE UNIVERSITY OF MICHIGAN
LIBRARIES
1817

POLICE PRACTICE
AND
PROCEDURE

BY

CORNELIUS F. CAHALANE

INSPECTOR IN CHARGE OF THE
TRAINING SCHOOL OF THE NEW YORK POLICE DEPARTMENT

WITH AN INTRODUCTION BY

ARTHUR WOODS

POLICE COMMISSIONER

WITH 12 ILLUSTRATIONS

NEW YORK
E. P. DUTTON & COMPANY
681 FIFTH AVENUE

The Knickerbocker Press, New York

INTRODUCTION

The author of this book, Inspector Cahalane, is in charge of the Training School of the New York Police Department. He is a practical policeman, having been through all the ranks of the force, and he has, to a marked extent, the habit of viewing police work in the light of the service it can render the community. I have thought so well of the book that it has been printed and distributed to all members of the force for their information and guidance.

The policeman's job is hard. He is exposed to all weathers, at all hours of the day or night. In emergencies he is on duty many extra continuous, wearing hours. He must grapple, without hesitation, with any situation that arises, no matter at what risk to life. He must be capable of using whatever degree of force may be necessary to capture outlaws; yet he must be courteous and considerate to civilians, even in the most irritating circumstances.

To do his difficult duty as he should, he must know the laws and ordinances—and they are legion; must know his duties, and the extent and the limitations of his powers; must be intimately acquainted with the ways of criminals, and thoroughly versed in the best methods of circumventing them. *Police Practice and Procedure* goes into all these matters better than any other book I know, and will be of the greatest value in clarifying the task of policemen and increasing their efficiency.

But the public should co-operate. They can help most

by learning enough of the working methods of criminals to be able to take intelligent preventive measures. A large percentage of the crimes committed in New York City are preventable. If civilians will read in this book the pages, especially, on crimes and criminals, and will take such reasonable precautions as suggest themselves, we shall all sleep safer, and the police force will be helped greatly in fulfilling its primary duty: the prevention of crime.

Arthur Woods,
Police Commissioner.

Police Headquarters,
November 25, 1914.

The information contained in this book is offered with the hope that it may instruct and assist the man on post and simplify his many duties. It has been gathered in the course of years of study and observation of police conditions. In its preparation I have become indebted to so many persons, in and out of the Department, who have specialized in particular branches of police work, that it would be impracticable for me to mention all their names, and I take this means of extending to them my sincere thanks for their assistance and advice.

CORNELIUS F. CAHALANE,
Inspector of Police,
City of New York.

TABLE OF CONTENTS.

CONTENTS

CONTENTS

CHAPTER I.

DISCIPLINE AND DEPORTMENT.

To obey strictly and execute promptly the lawful orders of superiors is one of the first requirements of the Department. Obedience is the foundation upon which all police efficiency is built. Without obedience to proper authority the force would be nothing more than a mob. It is a quality that is demanded from every member of the force, from patrolman to inspector. It is enough to know that the person giving the order is in proper command. He may be a man you do not like or respect, but you must omit the personal factor and respect his position and authority.

Orders must be *strictly* carried out. It is not enough to comply with only that part which you deem sufficient; nor is it proper or permissible when you are ordered to do a thing in a certain way for you to obtain the same results by other methods.

Orders must be *promptly* carried out. When an officer is given an order it is not for him to question its value or the manner prescribed for its fulfillment. When you understand just what the order calls for, carry it out immediately to the best of your ability and in a manner that admits of no misunderstanding.

Be loyal. The success of a squad, precinct or district depends greatly on the even teamwork of all its members. You should be for and not against the accomplishment of the functions of the Department, giving your most earnest and hearty support to those in authority. You cannot be loyal and be a knocker, a grumbler or a shirker.

Just one man of this type in a command is a nuisance and a centre of dissatisfaction. You should, therefore, discourage such tendencies in yourself and in those with whom you come into contact. Most grievances are fancied and the longer they are entertained, the greater they appear. If something is apparently interfering with you in the line of your duty and you feel that you are not getting a square deal, don't grumble—go to the person in immediate control and explain the circumstances and you will find that he can and will rectify any legitimate grievance.

Do not criticise the actions or orders of those placed in authority over you. You must assume that they are responsible, that they understand what they are trying to accomplish and have reasons for wanting things done in the way they prescribe. You must not assume that because you know of another way by which the same results might be obtained that they are wrong and you are right. Your superior officer will be judged by the final results obtained through such methods as he may pursue, whereas your responsibility ceases when you have carried out his orders.

The Police Department itself is often gauged by acts of its individual members. If you favorably impress persons they will judge the entire Department by that impression. Every officer, whether on or off duty, on patrol, in reserve, or at home, should, therefore, conduct himself in an exemplary manner. When in uniform, whether on or off duty, you are a target for the eyes of the public and if you do not conduct yourself in a gentlemanly manner you will be quickly observed. Do not do anything to attract attention unless it is necessary for the accomplishment of some police purpose. While in cars or other public conveyances, be particular to extend every courtesy. Do not occupy a seat while any other person is standing. Do not push, shove or jostle.

Do not do anything that is not gentlemanly. Do not spit on the sidewalk, cough in anyone's face, chew tobacco or gum, talk loudly or too much, or make unnecessary noise. Mind your own affairs and do not meddle with or critcise business people or other persons passing over your post. Refrain from influencing the business of any person.

It is better to talk too little than too much; an act committed or a story told by a private individual might be construed as idle and unimportant, but the same thing done by a policeman might become very significant. Idle gossip concerning yourself, the Department, or citizens, should not be indulged in, as a blasted reputation is seldom recovered and a gossipy man seldom makes a good policeman.

The matters you are prohibited from discussing, such as business of the Department, etc., you can avoid by frankly telling anyone who brings up the subject that you are forbidden by the rules of the Department to talk on such topics.

Do not shirk your duty. Leaving post unnecessarily and conversing are habits. Do not make appointments to meet persons on post; make them for times when you are excused from duty. Be particular about conversing unnecessarily with women while on duty.

In your home life, you and your family should conduct yourselves quietly and confine yourselves closely to the rules of decency and courtesy. Do not permit your wife and children to make use of your position as a veiled threat.

Excellent physique alone does not make the perfect policeman. He should possess sufficient strength of character, will power and moral courage to successfully resist any temptation to do wrong. Oftentimes persons engaged in undertakings requiring police supervision, or individuals of unsavory reputation will endeavor to induce you to overlook a violation of the law and may, if arrested, seek either directly or through friends to have you give weak or evasive testimony in court so that justice may be defeated. Be jealous of your character and reputation. Social companionship and intimate acquaintance with such persons should be carefully avoided, for in the majority of cases they seek your friendship with an ulterior object in view.

When you are on post in a section of the city populated by a foreign element you will find that you are expected by the people to be their doctor, their lawyer and their interpreter. You will be called upon at various times to render assistance in all good faith and confidence. Such confidence should not be betrayed or abused. You should do everything within reason to assist them, by summoning an ambulance surgeon, directing them to dispensaries, hospitals, the Department of Charities, the Legal Aid Society, etc. This you should do cheerfully and with the greatest possible attentiveness. If a person is sick and you are requested to assist him or her home, do so if it is within a reasonable distance in your own precinct or a short distance into an adjoining precinct, but always notify your station-house before leaving post.

Be courteous to everyone regardless of their position in life. Persons seeking assistance or advice are entitled to courteous and gentlemanly attention, and it is not courteous to be abrupt and short in your answers. You may be required to answer the same question a great many times during one tour if you are stationed in a congested section of the city and the repetition will become tiresome. Do not, however, lose your head or change your manner; the last person to ask a question is as interested in and as much entitled to the proper information as the first one. Do not appear surprised at the questions that are asked you; they may sound ridiculous to you but as a whole they are asked in good faith and warrant a courteous answer. Stand at attention and listen attentively to what they have to say, then give the best information or advice that you can. If you cannot supply the information they wish, direct them to some place where they may obtain it—to a store having a city or business directory, or, if the question relates to car lines, to a transfer agent or railroad inspector, etc. Do not think that you will be considered ignorant if you do not know the right answer to every question asked you, and do not give directions or advice unless you are sure you are right. The average person seeking advice will not feel offended if, being unable to help him yourself, you direct him to some place where he may get the desired information; but if you give him advice which he later discovers to be wrong, you can imagine his feeling toward you and the entire Department.

If you find some one who thoughtlessly or otherwise is about to violate a law or ordinance, warn him that such an act is illegal. If your warning is disregarded, take immediate and proper police action; if you do not, the disorderly element and even law-abiding citizens will look upon you as a man of weak, or even cowardly, character.

The early habits you form will remain with you as long as you are in the Department. If you are attentive to duty and courteous to persons with whom you come into contact during the first year you will continue so involuntarily throughout your career.

From the first tour of duty you perform, it should be your aim to prepare for the competitive examinations for promotion. Men who are ambitious for promotion make good policemen; they are attentive to their duty, jealous of their character and reputation, and as a result of their study of the rules and regulations, usages and customs of the Department, and the laws and ordinances, are mentally well equipped. There is an excuse for one man knowing how to do some one particular thing better than anyone else; he may have had to specialize at it. There is, however, no excuse for any police officer not knowing as well as any other man in the Department the rules and regulations and the laws and ordinances. The information is available and if one does not prepare himself on those subjects it is due to his own neglect and carelessness.

CHAPTER II.

PHYSICAL CONDITION.

When they enter the Department, patrolmen are fit to perform almost any physical task allotted to them in the line of their duty. This is due to their excellent physical condition, their youth and their training for the physical examination for appointment. After this appointment to the force, however, the arms and body get comparatively little exercise and therefore become stiff and accumulate fat, which brings with it a slovenly appearance and, very often, carelessness in dress and appearance.

It is natural for a policeman to gain and lose weight, but it should be gained and lost in all portions of the body, head, shoulders, arms, chest, legs, and not entirely in the abdomen, as is so often the case.

Obesity can be avoided by taking ordinary precautions; exercising all of the muscles and not a special few. A policeman should devote at least ten minutes a day, before eating, to exercise. On getting out of bed, he should open the windows wide, thoroughly ventilate the room, and take the calisthenic exercises taught in the School for Recruits. This will keep him in good physical condition. There is no more occasion for policemen to get stout than for soldiers in the United States Army. Their erect, soldierly appearance is due to daily exercise.

In standing, a policeman should not have his hands or arms folded or hanging in front of his body. This position throws the shoulders and head to the front. He should either place his hands on his hips or behind his back. His weight should be distributed equally on his feet. This prevents him from becoming lopsided. When he becomes tired, he can rest by shifting his weight to his toes and then to his heels.

Cause of Obesity

Cure for Obesity

Men who keep themselves in good condition will be found to be neat and to take pride in their appearance. As a result, their uniforms and equipments are always presentable. Patrolmen of this kind always command respect from the public. If an officer is snappy in appearance and commands respect for his office, and looks as though he were able to control any situation with which he might be confronted, he will not have to use one half the physical effort that a slow, careless or slovenly policeman would under the same circumstances.

Patrolmen should take particular care of their feet. Most foot troubles are due to the wearing of ill-fitting shoes; rundown heels, tending to cause the foot to press against that side, result in callouses and corns. When a condition of the feet exists that you cannot remedy, consult a chiropodist.

Due to police conditions, patrolmen lead irregular lives. Twice as much work is required at night as in the day, and in order that the work may be equally distributed, the force is divided into squads which rotate from day to night duty, a short period of time being allowed between the tours. This irregularity naturally breaks up and changes a man's mode of living, eating and sleeping. As a result, one is likely to not take sufficient time for rest and the mastication of his food. This seriously interferes with the digestive organs and tends to break down good health.

If you are excused for eight hours after having performed an eight-hour tour of patrol duty, rest during that interval so as to be fit during your next tour.

If you are ill, report on sick leave under the care of the police surgeon. Home, and not the street, is the proper place for sick policemen. The head of the Department, as well as the public, expects a patrolman on duty to be at his best. If you are sick on patrol, you may be called upon to perform the most strenuous act of your career, and to say that you failed because you were sick would be a lame excuse.

CHAPTER III.

PATROL.

Posts—Much of the success of the Department depends upon the manner in which patrol duty is performed.

A man going on patrol is like a man going to war, in that no matter how enthusiastic a soldier may be for the cause, if he is not able to shoot he is of little value; so with a man on patrol, unless he is rested, in good physical condition, properly equipped and uniformed, and understands how to cope with the conditions which will confront him, he too is of little value.

For the purpose of distributing the force, the Police Commissioner establishes what are known as posts. The length of such posts depends upon the police necessity of the section.

Fixed posts are established at intersections of streets in various parts of the city and are manned at night. Patrolmen are required to rotate to them at times designated and when so assigned, alternately do fixed post and patrol duty. When covering a fixed post you are required, while standing, to stay in the center of the post, but while in motion, you may walk anywhere within its boundaries.

If a person is discovered in the commission of a crime and an outcry is made, it should be impossible for him to escape if he keeps on the street.

Most householders living in the sections where fixed posts are in operation know that between 10 p. m. and 6 a. m. a policeman should be on the designated fixed post, and if they require your assistance they will call you. Many citizens have police whistles which they use in calling.

Special posts are established at designated places, such as fire ruins and cave-ins in the street. Men on such posts are expected to prevent unauthorized persons from entering the ruins and to keep pedestrian and vehicular traffic at a safe distance. Among other special posts may be mentioned raided gambling and disorderly houses, where an officer is stationed for the purpose of preventing the removal of evidence or a continuance of the nuisance; places where a serious crime has been committed; and premises where a strike has been declared, for the purpose of preserving the peace and preventing strikers from assaulting, threatening or annoying persons who are employed or seeking employment. Remember that the strikers are not violating the law when they *peacefully* request other persons to go on strike or not to take their places. The sidewalk and street at, or near, a strike must be kept clear for pedestrians and traffic.

Before going on patrol you are required to appear at inspection, uniformed and equipped as prescribed by the rules of the Department. You are then instructed as to all orders that relate to the performance of your duty. When directed, you will proceed to your post relieving point, where the officer you relieve will give you such information regarding the post as will assist you in performing your duty during that tour.

You will then start to patrol your post to the right; shield to the curb. This is done for the reason that your superior officers patrol to the left and should be able to find you readily if you are on post. If, however, you are suspicious of anything you should immediately turn back and try to verify your suspicion. At night or during the hours when business houses are closed you will try all doors, low windows and area gates, as explained under *Observation* on page 14.

While one portion of a post may require more attention than another, remember that a person planning a crime will always take advantage of the section of your post which he believes to be least patrolled.

If you are suspicious of any persons and it is necessary for you to stand in a doorway to watch, or if it is necessary to go into the hallway of a tenement for the purpose of examining the side door of a store, do so and inform the first visiting officer you meet.

Do not be timid about going anywhere in the vicinity of your post to perform proper police duty, through fear of being disciplined for being off post. Be sure, however, to comply with the rules defining what you must do when you leave post for a police necessity, in order that there may be no doubt as to the sincerity of your purpose.

When patrolling crowded thoroughfares keep on the outside of the crowd, that you may be seen. That is why you are dressed in a distinctive uniform. If you lose yourself in a crowd unnecessarily, you are temporarily useless.

At night, be suspicious of strangers who appear friendly and engage you in conversation. They may be interested in the commission of a crime on your post and endeavoring to hold you in conversation so as to permit their pals to escape. This also applies to persons who try to decoy you from your post, such as by telling you that you are needed immediately at some place. If you are suspicious take the person with you. Find out his name and address. If you find there is no truth in the complaint, make him accompany you, and examine your post immediately. If you find that a felony has been committed during your absence and you think he has decoyed you, arrest him on suspicion of being a principal in its commission.

The courts have held that the reputation of a place among the people living or doing business in the neighborhood is evidence of the character of the premises; that loud noise or anything injurious to public health or offensive to decency is contributory in establishing a nuisance.

It is sometimes difficult for the police alone to rid a community of a nuisance, and the complainants are generally unwilling to assist the Department, because of unwarranted fear of incurring the enmity of those in charge or because they wish to avoid loss of time in court.

If you can make them realize that no condition which is objectionable and in violation of the law can exist for any length of time if the residents in the block are determined to end it and are willing to sacrifice a little time, it should be easy to enlist their co-operation. Call to their attention the fact that in sections of the city where it is apparent, or where it has once been shown, that neighbors will not tolerate a disorderly condition, nuisances are never established.

If you have occasion to use a public telephone in communicating with the Department, as soon as the telephone company's operator answers, give her your name, rank, precinct and shield numbers before asking for your connection. When the Department's operator responds, identify yourself by giving your name, rank, precinct and shield number, and ask for the proper extension. If the matter is one which the operator will attend to, such as an ambulance call or a call for assistance, give the operator the number and location of the telephone from which you are talking, so that, if necessary, you may be sent for.

For assistance, give three or more blasts of your whistle, or three or more raps with your baton. If you are placed in such a position that you can use neither whistle nor baton, discharge your pistol in the air. If you hear a call for assistance give one signal with baton or whistle and run immediately in the direction from which the call came. In using your pistol to summon assistance, great care must be exercised for the safety of innocent persons. It is better to have the guilty person escape than to kill or injure an innocent bystander. There are times, of course, when it is not advisable to make a noise in summoning assistance, when, for instance, it might reveal your unsuspected presence. In such a case send someone in whom you have confidence for the help you need.

If it becomes necessary to leave your post, try to have the patrolman on an adjoining post cover it during your absence, and on your return make sure that nothing has gone amiss. Do not leave, except for a sufficient police or urgent personal reason. If you have a report, communicate with the station-house by means of the signal-box, or if one is not convenient, by means of a public telephone, and inform the lieutenant of the nature of the report. Be governed by his directions as to whether or not you will telephone it in or leave post and report it in person at the station-house.

Keep in harmony with the watchmen and special patrolmen on your post. If you have their co-operation they may render you valuable assistance.

Do not hound or persecute ex-convicts. If a man has been convicted of a crime and has paid the penalty, he is entitled to start life anew and should receive assistance and co-operation from you in his endeavor to live a decent life. If he lives on your post do not tell his neighbors of his past; if he is seeking employment, or is employed, do not inform the employer for the sole purpose of having him discharged. Tell your superiors or members of the Detective Division so that they may keep a watch on him. If he is hounded by the police and prohibited from engaging in a lawful vocation, there is only one door open to him, again to become a criminal.

Firearms—Use the utmost care in the handling of firearms at all times. Hold the weapon firmly, with the muzzle pointed to the ground, or in such manner that no person would be in the line of fire in case of accidental discharge. *Consider every gun loaded.*

Become thoroughly acquainted with the different types so that you may handle with safety to yourself and others almost any arm that may come into your possession. You should familiarize yourself with the action of the regulation revolver or pistol and learn to properly clean and oil it. Under ordinary conditions, the revolver or pistol should be cleaned and oiled at least once a month because, if neglected, dampness from perspiration will cause it to rust. It should be cleaned as soon as possible after having been discharged. One cleaning is generally sufficient after having used black powder cartridges, but when smokeless powder cartridges are used the arm should not only be cleaned as soon as possible after having been discharged, but again within twenty-four hours. Never attempt to clean or oil it without first making sure that the arm is unloaded. Take care that no oil runs onto the primers of the cartridges, as it may work into the powder and render the cartridges useless.

Use only cartridges suited to the arm.

The easiest and most accessible place to carry a pistol is in a holster, suspended from a belt, hanging on the left side toward the front of the body.

Form the habit of always removing your pistol and putting it in a safe place before undressing, so that it may not fall and be accidentally discharged.

A pistol, when not being carried, should always be secreted in some place where children cannot get it to play with and where a burglar or other intruder could not readily find it and arm himself.

Do not show your pistol to friends or others for the purpose of explaining its action. If any of them has a permit to possess a pistol he can learn from the dealer from whom he makes his purchase all he need know about it.

Do not draw your pistol at the slightest provocation or without cause; but in responding to a call for help or in searching a building or approaching the scene of a serious crime, such as a shooting or stabbing affray, have it in position for instant use.

In learning to shoot, or in practice, use an unloaded pistol. Stand easily, with the weight of the body balanced on both feet, the right foot a little in advance, and face slightly to the left. Grasp the handle lightly, so as not to cause trembling; raise the hammer with the thumb, close one eye, look through the groove of the rear sight until you see the front sight under the lower edge of the bullseye, and pull the trigger with a steady pressure—not a jerk. The position of the pistol after the hammer has fallen will show where the bullet would have struck had the arm been loaded. Practice will enable you to retain the aim and position during discharge. At the moment of firing do not shut the eyes and flinch. The secret of keeping the front and rear sights in line with the target as you fire, is to educate the muscles of the forefinger to act independently of those of the hand and arm.

Never try to shoot while running. Come to a full stop. Very few men can shoot effectively while they are in motion, and the chances are that some innocent person possibly two or three blocks away may be struck by the bullet.

Observation—A number of qualifications are required of a policeman. He must be strong, because he will be called upon to handle all kinds of people; fleet-footed, because he will be expected at times to overtake a fleeing culprit; courageous, because he must stand ready at all times to sacrifice his life in carrying out the functions of the Department; tall, because it will be necessary for him to see what is going on about him, sometimes over the heads of a crowd.

Unless he is observant, however, he may possess all these qualifications and still be almost useless as a policeman. In ten years he may not be called upon to run, use his strength or display his courage, but he is constantly called upon to use his powers of observation. The best policeman is he who is suspicious of everything that is going on about him. If everything always appears regular to him he will seldom, as a result of his own initiative, prevent crime. It is more essential from the taxpayers' point of view that crime be prevented, than that the perpetrator be detected and arrested. The city is put to considerable expense in convicting and imprisoning the guilty. If a policeman, by using his power of observation can prevent the commission of a crime he renders better service to the city than if he detects it. The best evidence of a patrolman's efficiency is the absence of crime on his post.

The best detectives are those who possess a keen sense of observation. In the Detective Division there are two grades; first grade, paying a salary equal to that of a lieutenant of police; and second grade, at the patrolman's ordinary salary. It should be an incentive to a patrolman to develop his observation, to know that assignment as First Grade Detective depends greatly upon results achieved by applying this sense.

To sharpen your observation, when assigned to a post for the first time, scrutinize the persons passing and try to gather from their carriage, actions and manner of dress what their occupations are; then make discreet inquiries to verify your deductions. Describe to yourself some person whom you have seen only once, his facial expression and complexion, wearing apparel, gait, etc., and when you see him again check up your description. By a little such practice you will be able, when necessary, to accurately describe some person whom you may have seen only casually.

Watch the vehicles passing over your post and note the names and business marks on them. In the case of motor vehicles practice memorizing the license numbers. Compute their speed by timing them over a given distance; in a short time you will become proficient in estimating it.

Do not be satisfied with simply taking the number of an automobile. If it has been used for the purpose of committing a crime or as a means of escape, the first or last number is likely to have been painted out. Familiarize yourself with the characteristic lines of the different models. It will, in most cases, narrow a search down to about five per cent. of the machines in use in the city if you report, for instance, that the car wanted is a "five-passenger 1914 X. Y. Z., blue, with no top."

In passing through a street, observe anything which seems unusual or out of place. Ask yourself: "Why is this? What is the reason for it? Is it regular? Does the person in charge of the premises know of this condition? Has he given permission?" Make inquiry of business men or householders. They will appreciate your inquiry when they know that your object is to protect them or their property, and though they may be inconvenienced by the inquiry they will commend you for the interest you have displayed in their behalf.

Watch persons entering and leaving buildings, particularly at night. If anyone arouses your suspicions, question him as to who he is and what business he had in the particular place. If his excuse is not satisfactory bring him back to the building for the purpose of identification.

In handling cases of this kind be careful of the manner in which you conduct yourself. If you are in uniform you need not tell your office, but if you are in civilian clothes your first words should be: "I am a policeman"; and you should display your shield conspicuously This is important because the ordinary person on being stopped at night by a man in civilian clothes will naturally assume that he is going to be held up and may run or, if he has a weapon, possibly assault you. An honest man will never find fault with a policeman for stopping him under these circumstances, provided it is done in a courteous manner. If your investigation proves that he was in the premises for a legitimate purpose you will find that he will commend rather than criticize.

In stopping a person under these circumstances always be on your guard. Take every advantage of him. Have your baton ready for instant use and be prepared to fight. If you are right handed keep him to the left. Keep close to his right hand and be ready to grab it in case he attempts to assault you. Remember that a person leaving a building after committing a crime anticipates being stopped and is usually prepared to give a better explanation of his movements (which, of course, will not stand investigation) than a person who has lawful reasons for being there. He will assault you if he believes that by so doing he can escape.

In searching or disarming a person possessing a firearm, extreme care should be taken that no opportunity is given him to use it on yourself or another. A search of this kind should be thorough, as men have been known to carry pistols sticking in the sides of their shoes, in the seat of trousers, on a spring fastened to the inside of a derby hat, up a coat sleeve and fastened to the forearm by rubber bands, and suspended by a cord around the neck and concealed beneath the coat and vest. Gangsters and men who consort with women of the street sometimes have the women carry their pistols for them. The woman generally has the pistol concealed in a muff, neck-piece, hand-bag, or the bosom of her dress.

Stop anyone with a bundle at night who is loitering in doorways or of whom you are suspicious. Find out the contents of the bundle. If he will not disclose what the bundle contains, arrest him on suspicion of being implicated in some felony which you are aware has been committed in the vicinity. This is legal; for, if a felony has been committed, you have reasonable grounds for believing that this person is the perpetrator, in view of the suspicious circumstances and his unwillingness to account for his movements or the contents of the package or bundle.

Be suspicious of persons entering buildings under the pretense of being canvassers, peddlers or agents, or representing themselves as inspectors or mechanics of the New York Telephone Co., the Department of Water Supply, Gas and Electricity, a gas company or the like. If in doubt, make them prove their identity. If they are what they seem, they will have no difficulty in doing so instantly. Should you have reason to doubt them further, make them accompany you and telephone to their office.

You should try to know by sight all persons living or doing business on your post. If possible, ascertain their business, time of arrival and departure. Where servants are employed, observe the persons in the habit of visiting them.

You will be called upon from time to time, by members of the Detective Division who are making investigations, for information regarding the character, habits and movements of persons on your post. If you are observant you can be of great assistance to them. Tell them all you know regarding the matter. You should be able to answer most questions of this nature.

Familiarize yourself with the locations and types of stores on your post, and as far as possible learn the stock carried, time of opening and closing, the persons usually attending to such duties, and the locations of safes, cash registers or property of value which could be readily stolen. Where lights are usually left burning, note their position.

On patrol at night, constantly try doors, low windows and area gates. It is often possible to so mark a window or door and its sill that a glance will tell you whether or not it has been tampered with. Where hanging locks or padlocks are used, on your first round turn them in such a manner that if they are disturbed while you have been on other portions of your post, you will know it the moment you see them.

When a store is found open, always get assistance. Try, if possible, to get the owner of the premises, or if his representative lives in the immediate neighborhood, send for him. Enter and examine it carefully. Note whether or not any of the property has been disturbed. If the place has been burglarized, search the premises for the perpetrator; he may be in hiding awaiting an opportunity to escape. As soon as possible notify the station-house.

If you do not believe that a crime has been attempted or committed, but find that the premises are open owing to some person's carelessness in not properly securing the door, close the place up. If necessary, use what is known as a "drop-lock"; get two sticks of wood, nail one to the floor and adjust the other so that, when the door is closed, it will act as a brace between the first stick and the door. Where there is a hasp use a police padlock, which can be obtained at the station-house.

In trying doors and windows, do not be satisfied with their appearance from the sidewalk. It will be found that after closing hours, when you have to depend entirely upon the light furnished by the street lamps, some portions of the block may be very dark and you cannot see from the sidewalk whether anything has been disturbed or not. It will be necessary for you to run your hand over the windows and sidelights in order to tell if they have been broken. Firmly shake all doors. If a pick-lock or false key has been used and the door left unlocked, you can discover it only by shaking the door and lock.

You should know the name and address of some person in authority in every store on your post who could be communicated with if it should be necessary to do so. If he does not reside on your post or conveniently near it, this notification must be made through the station-house.

Many business houses are equipped with burglar alarms. Sometimes these alarms are started by animals in the building and sometimes by weather conditions; nevertheless, you must investigate. If a burglar puts an alarm into operation and a policeman takes it for granted that there is no necessity for investigating, that officer is wilfully neglecting his duty.

If you find a street lamp not lit, but in a condition to burn, light it if possible. Be suspicious of lights on the street or in stores being extinguished suddenly. If you notice anything of this kind, make an immediate investigation; it may be the work of thieves.

Observe conditions surrounding vacant houses. If you learn that a building is about to be vacated, ascertain the name and address of the owner, where he can be communicated with, and the length of time the house will be empty. Report these facts to the station-house for record.

In vacant houses the principal item of theft is the plumbing. The thieves usually obtain entrance from the roof or through the cellar windows. Examine the sides and rear, in the case of a detached building, at various times during each tour. As a rule you can learn if any persons have been seen tampering with any particular building by inquiring of the occupants on either side, or in the rear.

Considerable property, especially in the winter, is destroyed by bursting water pipes. A policeman can readily detect such an occurrence by listening from the outside. If it be necessary at any time to enter a building for the purpose of protecting the stock, have the owner or his representative, if conveniently near, accompany you. Notify the station-house. Summon assistance and use sufficient force to enter the premises. Try to shut off the cock in the cellar; if this cannot be done, batter together the ends of the pipe with your baton, so as to lessen the flow of water.

When you smell gas escaping and life is in danger, summon assistance, force entrance if necessary, and render all possible aid. Open all doors and windows. Notify the station-house so that the Gas Emergency Patrol and a pulmotor may be sent if necessary.

Be on the lookout for dangerous street conditions, such as broken area gates, broken sewer manhole covers or conduit covers, bad holes in the sidewalk or street, or broken wires hanging from street poles. If anything of the kind is discovered, get assistance and guard it. Have the station-house notified. Place a barrel or planking in such a position that the danger is marked and guarded against. At night hang a lantern at the spot and see to it that it remains lit until daylight.

Pay particular attention to the frequenters of low liquor saloons, junk shops, second-hand dealers, curiosity shops, pawn shops and other places suspected of being "fences," where stolen goods are received and disposed of. If the things you observe do not call for action on your part, take a description of the persons you suspect and report the circumstances to the station-house for the information of the Detective Division.

Watch persons entering and leaving vehicles, especially any who appear to be intoxicated. They may be drugged or their companions may be thieves of the type known as "lush workers," who make a practice of robbing intoxicated persons. This applies equally to apparently intoxicated persons passing over your post.

A policeman patrolling without purpose, like an automaton, finds his work very tiresome and is constantly watching the clock or, in inclement weather, the thermometer. If the same effort is expended in observation for the purpose of preventing crime and detecting criminals, his tour will pass more quickly and with much more satisfaction to himself and to the Department.

Fires—One of the most important duties of a policeman is the prevention and detection of fires. You should be constantly on the alert. On the slightest suspicion, make a thorough and prompt investigation. Where life is in danger, as in an occupied or inhabited dwelling, particularly in the crowded sections of the city, promptly send in a fire alarm and signal for assistance. In such cases it is better to err by sending in an unnecessary alarm than to wait, and possibly have the Fire Department late in responding. When life is not in danger, be sure that there is a fire before sending in an alarm.

If you smell or see smoke or fire coming from a building and you are satisfied that there is a fire, or if someone shouts "fire" in a tenement and you cannot investigate without loss of time, you must promptly send in an alarm or make sure that one has been sent in. Do not be satisfied that someone else has done this unless you see the person actually sending the alarm or hear the mechanism of the box working, or unless another officer or some responsible person informs you that he has sent or witnessed the sending of the alarm.

The operation of the fire alarm signal-box merely registers in the Fire Department the location of the box, and they will respond to that point, expecting to find someone there ready to direct them to the scene of the fire. It is, therefore, necessary for an officer to remain at the box or to request some person of an age of discretion to do so, to intelligently direct the firemen.

In extremely cold weather the door of the fire signal box may be frozen and not respond to the turning of the handle. Do not hesitate to break the door to send the alarm.

After sending the alarm, run to the burning building; warn the occupants of their danger and assist them to the street. In doing this, be careful not to assist in the spreading of the fire by opening doors, windows or skylights and causing a draft. If it is necessary to open a door, be sure to close it again. Try as much as possible to close doors and windows instead of opening them, except for the purpose of saving life.

If you find a fire in a room, get the occupants out and close the doors and windows. For instance, if a fire occurs in a kitchen and the doors and windows are closed, it will take, possibly, ten minutes before the fire burns through the door, window or partition. If an alarm has been promptly sent, the apparatus of the Fire Department will arrive in two or three minutes in most sections of the city, and they can easily confine the fire to the room in which it started; but if skylights, cellar doors or windows are opened and a draft started, the fire and smoke will be forced into other parts of the building, and extend to the halls and stairways which must be used by the firemen in getting to the fire.

Upon the arrival of the fire apparatus, keep the crowd back, particularly from the entrances the firemen are using as a means of getting to and from the fire, and prevent persons from interfering with the firemen in the performance of their duties.

Fires are fought by the members of the Fire Department from the front and rear. In order to get to the fire quickly they stretch their lines from the streets and yards, consequently the fire lines must be quickly established on all streets and places where hose or other apparatus has been placed, so as to give the firemen free and uninterrupted use of the particular territory in which they are working.

When assistance arrives, keep the crowd beyond the last fire apparatus or hydrant to which hose is attached.

Be particular to permit no unauthorized person inside the fire lines or in the buildings in which the firemen are working. Take every precaution to guard property from theft during a fire.

Familiarize yourself with the design and color of badges and cards which authorize persons to enter the fire lines and ruins, and permit no person within the fire lines except members of the New York City Fire Department, and those having the proper badge or card conspicuously displayed.

Persons engaged in business within the fire lines, and who desire to go to their places of business, must be referred to a superior officer of the Police Department for this permission.

The Commanding Officer of the Fire Department at a fire is in command, and members of the Police Department must obey and respect any lawful order or suggestion that he may make.

Both departments must work in unison for the protection of life and property. The success of either in the accomplishment of their functions depends upon the promptness, skill, intelligence and even teamwork of both departments.

As soon as possible, secure the necessary information for a fire report, and, unless otherwise directed, send the information through signal-box to station-house.

After the Fire Department has left, prevent unauthorized persons from entering the fire ruins.

Accidents—When your attention is called to a person who is sick or injured, and who requires medical aid, summon an ambulance immediately. If a police signal-box is not conveniently near, use a public telephone and call the borough police headquarters, giving your name and precinct number, the number of the telephone you are using, and state the nature of the call, giving the location at which the ambulance is required.

If the patient is within a building, station some responsible person at the entrance to direct the ambulance surgeon.

While waiting for the ambulance, conform to the instructions issued by the Chief Surgeon of the Police Department on "First Aid to the Injured."

Obey any reasonable order or direction given by the ambulance surgeon and render him every possible assistance.

As soon as possible, obtain the pedigree of the injured person. Enter in your memorandum book exactly what he or she was doing just previous to the accident, such as, "Walking north, in front of —— Third Avenue," or "Crossing the street at 22d Street and Third Avenue, southeast corner to southwest corner"; enter the manner in which he or she was injured, the cause, the nature of the injuries sustained, the name and address of attending physician, the name and address of persons responsible (if the operator of a vehicle or car, the name and address of the operator and the name and address of the owner), and the names and addresses of witnesses.

This information is necessary for the Department's record. You are often required to testify as a witness, in case the injured person institutes a suit, and it is, therefore, essential that you have further data entered in your memorandum book, such as the distance of a car or vehicle from the curb and from the nearest street corner, its rate of speed, the number of persons near the scene, the persons handling or talking to the injured one, and anything peculiar to the accident.

If an accident occurs on the street (between house lines), the City of New York may be the defendant in a suit for damages. Be particular to observe the condition of the street or sidewalk, whether dry, wet, or slippery, whether the street lamps were lighted, the distance of street lamps from the point of accident, etc., and ascertain the destination of the injured person. Fill out an *accident report form* at the station-house.

In a case of this kind divulge no information concerning the accident to anyone except a superior officer, the coroner, district attorney or corporation counsel, or under due process of law.

First Aid to the Injured—On account of the hazardous nature of their calling and the accidents which they are likely to encounter, it is essential both for their own benefit and for the benefit of the public that all policemen have special knowledge of First Aid to the Injured. In emergency cases this knowledge enables policemen to put injured persons into doctors' hands in the best possible condition for cure. It also enables them to recognize the severity of an injury or illness. As a patrolman you will be called upon in such emergencies as burns, drowning, suffocation from smoke and gases, sunstroke, hemorrhage, poisoning, cases of people suddenly stricken with acute diseases and others.

The attention of every policeman is also earnestly invited to the great benefits to be had by studying how to *prevent* accidents as part of his instruction in First Aid.

In accident or emergency the policeman is the first official upon whom the handling of the case devolves, and it is especially essential that you be able to proceed in a confident, unhesitating and efficient manner. The bearing of an officer is very important, as by this you establish your efficiency or otherwise. You must proceed with decision, but without flurry, and be careful to avoid any appearance of excitement or undue haste; couple promptness with quiet efficiency. Retain your presence of mind and keep cool. Be ready to apply what you have learned and do so correctly and instantly. This is very important in order to secure proper handling of the condition, to inspire confidence in the injured and in others who may be present.

After assuring yourself that the situation warrants, or may possibly warrant it, send for medical assistance by calling an ambulance through your borough Headquarters. Remember that you are not a medical man and that your duty is simply to give such relief as the occasion demands until proper medical attention is obtained. Do not attempt too much; the interval before the arrival of the ambulance surgeon will probably be brief and your efforts must be confined to this period.

Having sent for the ambulance, study the situation, and if a crowd has gathered keep them from hemming in the patient, thus insuring plenty of fresh air and freedom from annoyance by remarks, questions and ill-timed advice. Nearly every bystander is of the opinion that he knows more about what should be done than any other and it is by your manner that you will show you are fully competent to command the situation.

Care of the Patient.

Place the patient flat on his back, with head slightly elevated, unless he is very faint, when the head should be placed quite low; put hands by side and gently extend legs.

If faint, keep the head low and give cooling drinks in summer or hot ones in cold weather; if at hand, aromatic spirits of ammonia, which has none of the disadvantages of alcohol. It is considered the best First Aid stimulant. The best way to give it is in teaspoonful doses in one-half glass of water.

An unconscious person cannot swallow, but he can inhale a stimulant. Under such circumstances the best stimulant is smelling salts, or water of ammonia. It is held under the nose so the patient may breathe its fumes. Cool sponging of face and head also helps faintness.

Do not give alcohol, except under the direction of a competent physician. Alcohol seldom does good and often harm, especially in hemorrhage, so that it is a good rule not to give it in First Aid.

An unconscious patient may vomit and, in doing so, may inhale solid matter into the air-passages and suffocate therefrom. To avoid this, turn the face well to one side so that the vomited matter will run out of the mouth.

Remedy any pressure from tight clothing, such as collar, shirt-band, tie or belt, that may interfere with breathing and circulation. If a woman, have some woman bystander assist to loosen the corsets.

If there is any reason to suspect broken or dislocated bones, be especially careful in handling the injured member.

Artificial Respiration.

Where breathing has been suspended for some time, artificial respiration should be applied as follows:

Loosen collar, belt or any clothing that binds the body.

Artificial respiration consists primarily in movements which alternately expand and contract the chest walls. This is accomplished by two methods.

First—The Schafer method. This possesses the advantage of not requiring the tongue to be held out of the mouth to prevent it from falling back into the throat. In this method the patient is placed face downward. The arms may be stretched straight over the head, or so placed that the patient's forehead is resting upon them. The face is placed to one side so that the air may be more easily inhaled and exhaled from the chest. The operator kneels at the side of the patient, or astride his body, but not resting upon it. He places his hands, palms downward, across the lower and movable ribs, then bends forward, and by the weight of his body and the pressure of his hands, contracts the chest walls and forces the air therefrom. The operator's body is then swung backward and the pressure on the elastic chest walls is relieved so that they expand and draw air into the lungs. These movements should be gradual and not so forceful as to produce injury. The time of pressure and of release should be equal and the movement should be repeated from fourteen to eighteen times per minute.

Second—The Sylvester method. The patient is placed upon his back. The tongue should be held out of the mouth by grasping it with a dry cloth or pincers. Place a pillow, rolled coat or some other available article under the shoulders. Kneel just above the patient's head, facing him and grasping his arms just below the elbows, pull the arms upward and outward to their fullest extent. Hold them thus for two or three seconds. This method expands the chest and forces the air into it. Then carry the arms downward and inward until the elbows are pressed firmly against the sides of the chest. Hold this position for two or three seconds and then repeat the operation described above. This should be repeated from fourteen to sixteen times per minute.

This method can also be applied with the operator kneeling across the loins of the patient, but not resting upon the body. In this position the operator pushes up the arms instead of pulling them up and pulls them down instead of pushing them down.

Artificial respiration should not be discontinued too soon, at least not under one-half hour, as many patients have been revived after a very lengthened period.

You will probably be called upon to use it in many emergencies, such as electric shock, suffocation by gases and drowning.

Shock

This is a condition so universally attendant upon injuries and severe mental excitement that your attention is particularly called to it.

Shock means a depression of the nervous system and may be so slight as not to be noticeable, or so severe as to cause death.

The skin is cold and covered with a clammy perspiration; the pulse is weak, rapid and irregular and the breathing shallow and infrequent. It differs from a fainting condition in that the patient is not unconscious.

Extend the patient upon his back, keep the head low, loosen collar, belt and tight articles of clothing.

If the injury permits, rub legs, arms and body, to restore circulation. Apply heat by means of hot plates wrapped in towels or flannels and placed over the stomach. Hot drinks should be given—tea, coffee, or aromatic spirits of ammonia (teaspoonful in half glass of water).

Stimulants *may* be administered by inhalation, such as smelling salts and water of ammonia held under the nostrils and inhaled. This is especially efficacious where the patient is unconscious.

ELECTRIC SHOCK.

In rescuing a person from a live wire you *must not touch the body unless you are insulated* (protected from electric current). The rescuer should cover his hands with rubber gloves, rubber coat or some other rubber substance, if it can be had; silk cloth may be wrapped about the hands, as silk is a non-conductor; or, a piece of dry rope may be used. Stand on a dry board or dry substance. *Never touch a person's clothing if it be wet.*

A live wire may be safely cut with an axe or hatchet having a dry wooden handle. A live wire may be removed from a patient by throwing it off quickly, using a dry board or stick, or your club. A patient may be pulled from a live wire by his own clothing providing it is dry and the ground around is dry. This should be done quickly so that the person may not receive repeated shocks.

A live wire may be short-circuited by dropping some metal substance across it, between the patient and the source of the current, one end touching the wire and the other the ground.

For after-treatment, see "Artificial Respiration" and "Shock."

SCALDS AND BURNS.

Scalds are produced by moist heat, and are caused by steam, hot water, etc.

Burns result from the exposure of the body to dry heat, such as fire.

In the case of either, the injury may be confined to the skin, or may extend deeper. With either of the injuries the great danger is shock.

If burns or scalds are extensive they need immediate hospital care. Before the arrival of medical assistance do *not* be too anxious to remove the clothing from the burned parts; remove only such as will come readily away without causing pain or disturbance of the burned surface. Such clothing as you do remove, *cut away* instead of pulling off. If possible, apply carron oil, which can be obtained readily from a drug store. If not obtainable, smear the surface freely with vaseline, olive or castor oil, fresh lard or cream, and exclude the air from the parts by covering with a clean linen handkerchief, towel or sheet. Do *not* disturb the patient more than is needful.

Intoxication—Alcoholic Coma.

One of the most common causes of coma is profound intoxication. Other causes are opium poisoning, apoplexy (the so-called stroke), injury to the brain, Bright's disease, ordinary epilepsy or fits, and a number of less frequent causes.

It is often very difficult even for a physician to distinguish between these various conditions, so it is apparent that the policeman should seldom attempt it. Errors of judgment in this matter (considering a person intoxicated and putting him in a cell when he is suffering from some more serious condition) are of too frequent occurrence and subject this Department to just and very serious criticism.

In the coma of alcohol the unconsciousness is seldom so deep as in other conditions, and the person can generally be aroused by the infliction of some slight pain. The odor of alcohol is not to be depended upon, as a sick person may have taken it on feeling ill or faint.

Whatever the cause when persons are unconscious they had best be taken to the hospital for further observation or at least the responsibility should be put up to the ambulance surgeon.

Drowning and Suffocation From Smoke, Gases, Etc.

These two cases are somewhat similar and will be discussed together.

The chief difference is that in drowning, it is water, in suffocation, smoke and irritating gases (chemical, illuminating, etc.), that prevent the entrance of air into the lungs.

In cases of drowning the main points are to get the water out of the lungs and to cause the patient to recommence breathing.

To remove water from the lungs strip the patient quickly to the shirt or undershirt and wipe all frothy mucous from the throat and mouth with a handkerchief. Place patient on the ground, face downward, and grasping him under the hips raise him up and down several times, thus allowing the water to run out of the mouth.

Do not use much time at this, but proceed at once to *artificial respiration.* With the Schafer method it will not be as necessary to get out the water as with the Sylvester method.

In suffocation from illuminating gas, etc., proceed at once to the application of artificial respiration while awaiting arrival of ambulance with pulmotor.

Cat and Dog Bites.

Call an ambulance and while awaiting its arrival tie a string, handkerchief or bandage between the bitten part and the body, if practicable. The cutting off of the return of the blood to the body limits absorption from the wound. The wound should then be soaked in hot water, if obtainable, and, in any event, squeezed or sucked. In this way the poison is extracted. This treatment should not be delayed for a moment. A red-hot piece of iron wire or steel may be used for burning the wound. Strong ammonia or nitric acid may also be used for this purpose. When the wound is cauterized the constricting band may be removed and the wound dressed. These extreme steps should be taken only in cases where medical assistance is not immediately obtainable.

Poisons.

This treatment consists in a general way of three steps:

First—Attempt to dilute the poisonous substance so that it may be less concentrated, caustic and dangerous. For this purpose milk is generally available and can be given in almost any poisoning; or three or four raw eggs may be administered.

Second—Then attempt to change the poison taken into a harmless substance by some remedy (i. e. an antidote).

Third—Attempt to remove the poison from the stomach by some remedy which will produce vomiting, using what is called an emetic.

Many poisons themselves produce vomiting. If the patient has already begun vomiting and is conscious, cause him to drink lots of water which will assist in removing the poison from the stomach. This is better given lukewarm. With it may also be given the soothing substances mentioned above; milk or egg.

If the patient is not vomiting, a handy emetic is mustard, one or two teaspoonsful of which stirred quickly in a glass of water may be given. Putting the finger down the throat will often induce vomiting. Later the doctor will use the stomach pump.

Carbolic poisoning, give as much milk as you can get the patient to take, at least one or two pints. Or, give him three or four raw eggs quickly stirred in water. This is to dilute the poison. Then give epsom salts, which can generally be handily obtained. This is the very best antidote for carbolic forming with it a compound which is quite harmless.

Next in value is strong alcohol, such as whisky, brandy or proof spirits. In cases of external carbolic burns, apply pure alcohol which will at once arrest further action of the acid.

Use the remedy which you can get most quickly—a bottle of milk in a restaurant or dairy; epsom salts in a drug store, etc. In any case, act quickly.

For *oxalic acid*, give lime in some form, mixed with water. If you can't get it any other way, scrape off white-wash or plaster from the wall, stir it up in water and give at once.

For *mineral acids*, give at once an alkali, such as soap, chalk, magnesia.

For *caustic alkalies*, give a considerable amount of a dilute acid, such as vinegar in water.

Sunstroke and Heat Exhaustion.

In the summer during protracted hot spells you may be confronted by one or the other of these conditions. The symptoms differ in the two.

Sunstroke proper. The person is generally unconscious. The skin is exceedingly hot and dry, and the face flushed. The pupils of the eyes are small. The breathing is generally very labored and noisy. The fever is very high.

The problem is to lower this fever. Apply pieces of broken ice to the head and wrists. Rub the chest and back with ice or cold water. Remove person to as cool and shady a place as possible.

Heat exhaustion. Patient also unconscious, but less deeply so. The skin is apt to be cool and moist. There may be no external appearance of fever. The face is pale. The breathing is usually slow and sighing.

Apply warmth. Give a stimulant (aromatic spirits of ammonia, a teaspoonful in one-half glass of water).

Freezing and Frostbite.

Restore warmth to the body gradually. The patient should not be taken into too warm a place, or too much warmth applied at once. Rub the limbs and body to restore circulation by friction and gradually increase the heat applied to the body. As soon as you are able, give warm drinks, such as tea, coffee or aromatic spirits of ammonia.

In cases of freezing *never* take a person directly into a hot room or directly apply heat.

Whenever a particular part is frozen and there is no general freezing, rub the part with snow, ice or cold water.

Never apply heat at first.

Fractures.

Send for an ambulance immediately and make the patient as comfortable as possible. Do not move the patient unless it is absolutely necessary as this may result in injury from moving the sharp ends of the bone.

There are two kinds of fractures: simple and compound. In a simple fracture the skin is not broken. In a compound fracture, which is more serious, the skin is broken and air is brought in contact with the bones through the torn tissues.

Be very careful in the manipulation of fractures, especially simple ones, or you may readily convert a simple fracture into a compound one, which is a very serious matter.

Compound fractures may be rendered much more complicated by unnecessary movements and, as fractures may be set as readily after some hours have elapsed, do not interfere unnecessarily. See that the wounds of compound fractures are kept as clean as possible. In fractures of the upper extremities the patient generally supports it himself in such a way as to give him the least discomfort. In fractures of the lower extremities, place the patient on his back and gently stretch the limb out, if this is possible. If it causes too much pain, let him alone. You may, however, support the limb on each side with pads, such as a folded coat or pillow.

After a fall on the head, bleeding from the ears, nose and throat and into the whites of the eyes generally means that there is a fracture of the skull. Such a patient is generally unconscious. There is nothing you can do in this condition except to look after his comfort.

Epilepsy.

Epilepsy, commonly known as "fits," is a condition that you will frequently be called upon to look after. This will usually be recognized by the twitching and convulsive movements of the muscles of the face and body, the frothing at the mouth and grinding of the teeth; the froth is often bloody because the tongue or lips have been bitten.

The patient is unconscious and helpless. The convulsions come on suddenly and nothing can be done to stop them. See that the patient is kept upon his back with the head low. To prevent injury to head or limbs, restrain the patient from threshing around, and insert a cork, handkerchief, or some substance (not too hard) between the teeth to prevent laceration of the tongue.

The fits do not last long, but *send for an ambulance*, as there may have been injuries occasioned by the fall.

Hemorrhage.

This means bleeding from any cause. It may be moderate, in which case it will stop itself; it may be severe and require immediate attention. It may be internal and invisible, in which case you can do nothing, or visible and external, in which case you can help. Many lives have been saved by the work of intelligent policemen.

Practically the only bleeding in which you can be of assistance is that of the extremities, the leg or arm, in which case several methods are available.

Where the blood vessels in the body are intact there is no greater tendency for the blood to settle at the lower points of circulation than at the higher, but if this continuity is broken by a wound of the artery the balance is destroyed and the blood tends to settle down to the lower part. Therefore, an elevated position of the part will oftentimes stop hemorrhage, or help to stop it. Thus, in a wound of the foot or arm the patient should be *laid upon the back and the affected limb raised.* In a wound of the hand or arm the patient should preferably be seated and the *limb raised.* Likewise, in bleeding from the head the patient should sit or stand up.

Pressure is the most commonly applied method of stopping bleeding. It may be exerted directly upon the wound or by a plug in the wound; in the case of arterial hemorrhage by constricting the limb between the wound and the body; in bleeding from the veins, by constricting the limb beyond the wound.

Pressure directly applied to the bleeding part with a folded towel or handkerchief (always get as clean a piece of cloth as possible), and continued firmly and steadily for some minutes will generally control the bleeding. Pressure may be exerted upon the wound or upon the entire limb above the wound, that is, between the wound and the body, or upon the injured blood vessel itself between the wound and the body.

Nearly every case of hemorrhage may be controlled by direct pressure of the fingers upon the bleeding point.

A clean piece of cloth inserted in the wound in the form of a plug or compress and firmly held in place will in a great majority of cases stop bleeding. This plug or compress should, if possible, extend out of the wound so that it may readily be held in place. The hands are apt to become tired through continued pressure and this plug or compress may be held in place by a handkerchief or piece of cloth and a bandage tied over it. This method may be applied to any bleeding wound.

There is an instrument called a "tourniquet," which is designed to go around an arm or leg and with the turning of a screw constrict the leg or arm by pressure so that the blood cannot flow through the vessels.

A tourniquet may be improvised by constricting the extremities with a rope, rubber pipe, handkerchief, a strong piece of cloth, or, you might use your belt. The circulation of an extremity may be more effectually stopped by placing a stick under the rope, or whatever is used, and twisting it around so as to accomplish more complete constriction.

You should bear in mind that *the constriction of a part by this method for too long a time might cause permanent injury* to the limb through completely cutting off circulation from the parts below and thereby causing mortification.

To expose the bleeding part, rip the clothing up the seams with a scissors or knife, and avoid exposing more than is necessary.

Pressure by some hard body, such as a bottle, stone or tightly folded cloth may be made in the joint next above the bleeding point and the limb bent upon it firmly and held in that position. For instance, if the wound is below the elbow joint some firm substance may be placed in front of the elbow joint and the arm brought up and placed firmly against it and held there.

Bleeding from the large *veins* may be distinguished by its darker color and steady flow, from the more severe bleeding of the arteries, which is deep red in color and spurts out at regular intervals with the beat of the heart. This is not usually severe, but in case it is, apply pressure quickly to the wound as described above or constrict the limb below the wound. that is, on the side farthest from the body.

In a case of hemorrhage from the lungs, place the patient in a *recumbent* position and give a teaspoonful of common salt, dry.

In nose bleed, which may be so severe as to cause anxiety, cold water or solutions of salt or alum may be snuffed up into the nostrils. If these are not efficacious the nostrils must be plugged with cheese cloth or old linen. Take a strip half an inch wide and push it up into the nostrils with a penholder or pencil and allow the end to hang out of the nose. *This should only be done before the arrival of the ambulance surgeon when the case is very severe and the danger great.*

NEVER GIVE ALCOHOL to a patient suffering from hemorrhage.

CHAPTER IV.

ARRESTS.

For the purpose of placing responsibility and to prevent confusion of power, the system of government in this State has been divided into three branches:

First—Legislative, consisting of the Senate and the Assembly. Its duty is the making of laws for the State. The Board of Aldermen is the legislative branch of the city government.

Second—Judiciary, comprising the courts of the State. Its duties are to interpret the laws and to punish transgressors.

Third—Executive, or administrative, of which the Police Department is a part. Its duties are to prevent violations of the law and to bring before the judiciary for punishment, in the manner prescribed by the legislative branch, those who do violate the law.

It is specifically provided that one branch cannot usurp the powers of any other branch.

If you find a condition which you believe is not right, and you know that it has not been prohibited by the legislature, you cannot make your own law to fit the case.

If a person commits a prohibited act, the power to punish is vested in the judiciary. For instance, if you apprehend a murderer, you must not unnecessarily strike him no matter how mean or contemptible he may be. If you do you are usurping the power of the judiciary. Remember that under the law all persons are assumed to be innocent until proven guilty in the manner provided, and if you punish you are taking away from that person the rights he is guaranteed by the Constitution—that he may not be punished for an offense until proven guilty, after an opportunity has been given him to present his defence.

A crime is an act or omission forbidden by law.

A warrant is an order in writing, signed by a magistrate, commanding a peace officer to arrest the person named therein.

Sec. 151 Form No. 68.

First Division, City Magistrates' Court, 1st District.

CITY AND COUNTY OF NEW YORK, } ss.:

In the name of the People of the State of New York: To the Sheriff of the County of New York, or any Marshal or Policeman of the City of New York:

WHEREAS, Complaint in writing, and upon oath, has been made before the undersigned, one of the City Magistrates for the City of New York, by *John Jones* of No. *35 Bleecker* Street, that on the *10* day of *August* 19*14*, at the City of New York, in the County of New York, the following article, to wit: *One case of dry goods*

of the value of *Forty nine 00/100* Dollars, the property of *Brown and Company and in care & custody of deponent* was taken, stolen or carried away, and as the said complainant has cause to suspect, and does suspect and believe, by *Edward Burns*

WHEREFORE, the said Complainant has prayed that the said Defendant may be apprehended and bound to answer the said complaint.

THESE ARE, THEREFORE, in the name of the PEOPLE of the State of New York, to command you, the said *Sheriff, Marshals and Policemen*, and every of you, to apprehend the body of the said Defendant, and forthwith bring *him* before me, at the *1st* DISTRICT CITY MAGISTRATES' COURT, in the said City, or in case of my absence or inability to act, before the nearest or most accessible City Magistrate in this City, to answer the said charge, and to be dealt with according to law.

Dated at the City of New York, this *1* day of *Sept* 19*14*

William Smith
City Magistrate.

FIRST DIVISION.

City Magistrates' Court, ______ District

THE PEOPLE, ETC.,
ON THE COMPLAINT OF

John Jones

vs.

Edward Burns

WARRANT—LARCENY.

Dated Sept 1- 1904

William Smith City Magistrate.

John Brown Officer.

The Defendant Edward Burns taken and brought before the Magistrate to answer the within charge, pursuant to the command contained in this Warrant.

John Brown Officer.

Dated Sept. 7. 1904

This Warrant may be executed on Sunday or at night.

William Smith City Magistrate.

43 A-61, '09, 3,000 (P)

A subpœna is an order in writing, signed by a magistrate, district attorney or clerk of a court, commanding the person named therein to appear at the place designated to give information on a matter to be inquired into.

FORM No. 178
SUBPŒNA

CITY MAGISTRATES' COURT, 5th DISTRICT, FIRST DIVISION

CITY AND COUNTY OF NEW YORK, } ss.:

In the Name of the People of the State of New York

To William Smith

No. 149. Jones Street.

YOU ARE COMMANDED to appear before me

one of the City Magistrates in The City of New York, at the 5th District City Magistrates' Court, 114, E 171st st

in the said city, on the 14 day of May 1914,

at 10 o'clock in the fore noon of that day, as a witness in a criminal action prosecuted by the People of the State of New York against John Doe

and for a **Failure to attend** you will be deemed guilty of a Criminal Contempt, and liable to a **Fine of Two Hundred and Fifty Dollars** and **Imprisonment** for thirty days.

Dated at The City of New York, this 17 *day of* May 1914

David Jones
City Magistrate.

65 a-54-13 (B) 15,000

A summons is an order in writing, signed by a magistrate, commanding the person named therein to appear at the court designated for the purpose of answering a charge.

No. 272201
May 4 1914
Name of Defendant John Smith
Address 14 E 91st St
Returnable 9 Am
May 5th 1914
Officer John Doe
Precinct 15th
{this stub to remain in book}
Form 177a

No. 272201
May 4 1914
Name of Defendant John Smith
Address 14 E 91st St
Returnable 9 Am
May 5th 1914
Officer John Doe
Precinct 15th
{this stub to be delivered to desk officer}
Form 177a

Form 177a

SUMMONS No. 272201

CITY MAGISTRATES' COURT, 4th DISTRICT, FIRST DIVISION

In the Name of the People of the State of New York:

To John Smith

You are hereby summoned to appear before the 4th District City Magistrates' Court, No. 151 E 57 Street, Borough of Man., City of New York, on the 5 day of May 1914 at 9 o'clock in the fore noon, TO ANSWER a charge made against you by Police Officer John Doe of 15th Precinct, for violation of Sanitary Code, and upon your failure to appear at the time and place herein mentioned, you are liable to a fine of not exceeding FIFTY DOLLARS, or to IMPRISONMENT of not exceeding TEN DAYS, or both.

Dated at The City of New York, this 4 day of May 1914.

Attest: John Doe Police Officer,
15th Precinct.

William McAdoo
CHIEF CITY MAGISTRATE.

8881 10 (B) 100,000

An arrest is the taking of a person into custody that he may be held to answer for a crime.

A person is in custody under the law when he is placed under restraint or when he submits to same.

A patrolman cannot release a prisoner after having arrested him.

An attempted crime is an act done with intent to commit a crime and tending, but failing, to effect its commission. To determine the particular crime attempted you ask yourself: "What would this person have been guilty of if the attempt had been successful?" For instance, if you caught a man who, with a lighted match in his hand, had been trying to set fire to a building, but no fire occurred, it should be apparent to you that he must be charged with attempted arson.

Crime is divided into two broad classes—felonies and misdemeanors. For your purpose you need only know that a felony is any crime the penalty for which is death or imprisonment in a State Prison, and that a misdemeanor is a crime punishable, upon conviction, by imprisonment in a county jail, penitentiary or city prison, by fine up to the amount of $500, or by both.

A principal to a crime is one who commits a crime, or who aids, advises, counsels or assists in its commission. If one person tells another where he can commit a crime, explains how to do it, or knowingly provides him with the tools required in its commission, he is a principal. If he stands on watch for another while that person is committing a crime, he is a principal.

An accessory is one who after a felony has been committed, harbors, conceals or hides the perpetrator, with intent to prevent his arrest. In misdemeanors all concerned are principals.

It is not necessary for you to know the exact Penal Law definition of each crime, but you should know the elements that go to make up each crime. It is often difficult for the court, after having heard all of the evidence and with a law library to consult, to settle on the degree of crime a prisoner has committed. You must, however, be able to distinguish a felony from a misdemeanor almost as readily as you can tell your shield number, because you have power of arrest in one case that you do not possess in the other. In crimes where the degrees are divided into classes, such as grand and petit larceny, felonious and simple assault, and abandonment, you must be able to distinguish each class before you can take intelligent action.

In making arrests under a warrant you are governed by the following sections of the Code of Criminal Procedure:

"SECTION 170. If the crime charged be a felony, the arrest may be made on any day, and at any time of the day or during any night. If it be a misdemeanor, the arrest cannot be made on Sunday, or at night, unless by direction of the magistrate indorsed upon the warrant."

"SEC. 173. The defendant must be informed by the officer that he acts under the authority of the warrant, and he must also show the warrant, if required."

"SEC. 169. Every person must aid an officer in the execution of a warrant, if the officer require his aid and be present and acting in its execution."

"SEC. 155. If the warrant be issued by a justice of the supreme court, recorder, city judge or judge of a court of general sessions in the city and county of New York, or by a county judge, or by the recorder of a city where jurisdiction is conferred by law upon such recorder or by a judge of the city court, it may be directed generally to any peace officer in the State, and may be executed by any of those officers to whom it may be delivered."

"SEC. 156. If it be issued by any other magistrate, it may be directed generally to any peace officer in the county in which it is issued, and may be executed in that county; or if the defendant be in another county, it may be executed therein, upon the written direction of a magistrate of such other county indorsed upon the warrant, signed by him with his name of office, and dated at the city, town or village where it is made, to the following effect: 'This warrant may be executed in the county of Monroe,' (or as the case may be)."

In the City of New York, under the Inferior Courts' Act, a warrant issued by a city magistrate may be executed in any county in the City of New York without further indorsement.

It is determined from the offense described in the warrant whether the case is a felony or a misdemeanor.

The warrant must be delivered to the court in which the prisoner is arraigned.

A peace officer without a warrant has no more power than a private individual in making an arrest for a misdemeanor.

A non-resident may be arrested in this State for a crime committed out of the State on receipt of a telegram from the authorities of the place where the crime was committed, provided a felony is charged.

When you know that a warrant has been issued for a person charged with a felony, and you have not the warrant in your possession, you may arrest that person under Section 177 of the Code of Criminal Procedure, in that a felony has in fact been committed and you have reasonable grounds for believing that the person to be arrested committed it.

When your attention is called to the commission of a crime you must act quickly. Usually you cannot consult a reference or get advice as to your powers. You must be right. It is a serious offence as well as a great injustice to the person accused to make an illegal arrest. As a rule, when anything happens to a person he looks around for a policeman; finding one, he demands the arrest of the person complained of, regardless of whether or not it is lawful. When you are approached by such a complainant, listen to what he has to say, and if his story is not clear, ask questions to bring out the material facts. Let him do the talking, you the questioning and listening. If he wants a person arrested, ask yourself: "Does the substance of the complaint constitute an act or omission forbidden by law?" If it does not, inform him that you cannot take any action; if he wants to know your reason, tell him frankly. If it does, see if it comes within any of the four provisions of the Code of Criminal Procedure wherein you are permitted to make summary arrest, viz.:

"SECTION 177. A peace officer may, without a warrant, arrest a person:

1. For a crime, committed or attempted in his presence;
2. When the person arrested has committed a felony, although not in his presence;
3. When a felony has in fact been committed, and he has reasonable cause for believing the person to be arrested to have committed it."

"SEC. 179. He may also, at night, without a warrant, arrest any person whom he has reasonable cause for believing to have committed a felony, and is justified in making the arrest, though it afterward appear that a felony had been committed, but that the person arrested did not commit it."

If one person charges another with the commission of a *misdemeanor* not committed in your presence, and it is not plain from the facts that a misdemeanor has been committed, refer the complainant to the district court. If it is apparent that the accused has committed a misdemeanor, inform the complainant that he may arrest him and that you will convey his prisoner to the station-house. The complainant need not touch the prisoner; he may simply tell him that he is under arrest.

If you are accosted by a civilian and he delivers someone to you whom he has already placed under arrest, under the law you must take his prisoner to the station-house.

In either case, get the name and address of the person making the arrest and have him accompany you to the station-house. Be careful to see that his name is entered on the Department's records as having made the arrest and that he signs and swears to the complaint in court.

If you are requested by some one claiming to be a peace officer to assist in making an arrest and he is not known to you, insist upon seeing his badge of authority. If he is executing an order of a court, such as a warrant or summons, make him show you the document. If it is a warrant issued by a police magistrate outside of the City of New York, see that it is indorsed by a magistrate for service in the county within which the arrest is to be made.

Under the Inferior Courts' Act, a peace officer may make arrests upon the presentation of a form issued by the Domestic Relations Court which is given the peace officer by the complainant, who must identify the person to be arrested.

Identify and summon persons who commit petty offenses *except* those who are intoxicated or charged with larceny or malicious mischief (such as breaking windows or otherwise destroying property), or who are engaged in a serious breach of the peace (acting in a disorderly manner on cars or annoying or interfering with others on the street); and also in cases of complaint where you do not witness the violation.

Do not make petty arrests. It usually suffices to warn persons if they are committing some little infraction of the laws or ordinances, but if anyone persists after being warned, arrest him.

Certain persons, such as ambassadors representing foreign countries, are immune from punishment in the United States, but they are not immune from arrest. Such a person, if arrested for a serious offence, would be returned to the country he represents for trial.

If a bondsman wishes to surrender a prisoner to you, ask him if he has a surrender order from the court. If he has not, tell him to arrest the person and that you will protect him while doing so. The prisoner must be taken to the station-house and from there to the place where he would be confined if not on bail.

While children are arraigned in a Court of Special Sessions (Children's Court), the Court of Special Sessions will recognize a summons issued by a magistrate.

Do not arrest a child without sufficient provocation. It is very likely to do more harm than good, unless the offence is a serious one.

Do not arrest persons for threatening you unless there is some other provocation which constitutes a breach of the peace.

You will, from time to time, be called into a building by one member of a family to settle a dispute. Usually it is the wife, who claims that her husband has struck or threatened her or some member of the family. In the majority of cases the matter could easily have been settled without police interference, and if you tell her to go to court and lay the facts before a magistrate, the affair will be amicably settled before she has time to do so. If, however, she claims that there are young children in the house and their lives are in danger because of the condition of their father or others, go with her and if, from appearances, her apprehensions are justified, inform her that she may arrest her husband and that you will take him to the station-house.

Every person must be informed of the reason for his arrest unless he is arrested in the actual commission of a crime or after a chase immediately following.

You are prohibited by law from taking any action in civil cases except to preserve the peace. For instance, if someone has a civil process to serve and he anticipates being assaulted, under those circumstances you must go with that person to protect him and to prevent a breach of the peace. Permit no one to use your office in coercing another in the execution of a civil process.

In making an arrest, if you have reason to believe that the prisoner has a weapon on his person, give him a superficial search by feeling his pockets. If he has a weapon call some person to witness your taking it from his person, and if it has been carried in violation of the law make an additional charge against him in court. It is a safe rule to put the nippers on every man who is charged with theft or who is likely to attempt to escape or to assault you. If you are right handed, put the nippers on the prisoner's right hand and hold them with your left. This permits you to carry your baton in your right hand and to protect yourself in case of assault.

If a prisoner is likely to have any evidence on his person, see that he does not dispose of it on the way to the station-house. Do not permit him to put his hands in his pockets, throw anything into the street, or give anything to his friends.

It is natural to expect that a person placed under arrest will become excited and lose his temper—possibly threaten you. There is, however, no excuse for you to lose your head or to get excited.

Prisoners partly intoxicated will want to fight and you may experience difficulty in getting them to the station-house. It is cowardly, as well as a violation of the law, to strike a prisoner unless your life is in danger or he is trying to escape. If you must strike a prisoner, strike him on the wrists or legs rather than on the head. Endeavor to put into practice the humane manner of handling prisoners as taught in the School for Recruits.

If you are followed to the station-house by a crowd, do not let your attention be diverted from your prisoner. If you feel that you are likely to be assaulted or that your prisoner may escape, summon another policeman, if possible, or command any person present to assist you.

Do not summon a patrol wagon unnecessarily. If a prisoner lies down and refuses to move, coax him. If there is no physical reason why he should not walk and his condition is not offensive to public decency, use sufficient force to make him walk to the station-house if the distance is not too great.

Wherever you are permitted to make an arrest, you are allowed to use sufficient force to effect it. You may break open a door or window to enter a building but you must first announce that you are a peace officer and that you want the door or window opened for the purpose of arresting "John Doe" or whoever it may be.

CHILDREN.

Children, under the law, are persons actually or apparently under the age of sixteen years, except where the sale of liquor is involved, when the age is eighteen years.

All children arrested, under the age of sixteen years, shall be charged with Juvenile Delinquency, *except*

1. When conviction might result in capital punishment.
2. When the act, if committed by an adult, would not be criminal. (Entering a theatre without the consent of guardian, smoking or buying cigarettes, entering pool parlors, etc.)

A child taken into custody under circumstances coming within this second exception cannot be charged with Juvenile Delinquency; it must be charged with Improper Guardianship, for the reason that the law provides that every guardian of a child must exercise proper care and control over a child to prevent it from violating the law or requiring the care or attention of the State.

It is the policy of the Legislature and of all persons interested in the well-being of children to prevent their contact with hardened criminals. They have, accordingly, provided separate places of detention, means of conveyance and arraignment for children to keep them from associating with or forming the acquaintance of adult criminals. The law provides that a child, while under restraint or conviction, shall not be placed in any place of confinement or in any vehicle in company with adults who are charged with crime. It further provides that it shall be the duty of officers having a child in charge to notify the parent, guardian or custodian of such child, and with all convenient speed to take such child to the Children's Court, if in session; if not in session, then to the rooms of the Society for the Prevention of Cruelty to Children, provided bail has not been accepted or recognizance taken.

Never scare or threaten children, or permit other persons to scare children by threatening to have a policeman punish them. Do not unnecessarily interfere with children engaged in innocent amusement. If it is necessary to speak to children to prevent their doing something which is a violation of the law or an inconvenience to persons or injury to property, do so in a kindly manner; if that does not suffice and their parents are conveniently near, speak to the parents. This generally suffices to correct most of these complaints. If children, in this way, are taught that a policeman is their friend, it will not be possible for them to be lost for any extended period. They cannot wander far without meeting a policeman, and if they are not afraid of him, they will immediately tell him of their troubles. In innumerable cases it has been found that lost children had hidden in doorways on the approach of a policeman, having been led to fear him.

Unless it is absolutely necessary, do not take action which will separate children from their parents, for unless the mother is a prostitute, thief or drug fiend, she is, as a rule, the best person to take care of her own children. Do not separate a nursing baby from its mother unless the health or life of the child is endangered.

Foundlings are abandoned children under two years of age. If you have to do with a foundling, try to arrest the person responsible for the abandonment. Take the finder and foundling to the station-house so that the former may make the affidavit required by the Department of Charities as a means of identification.

Abandoned children over two years of age are considered as "lost children." Make diligent inquiry to find the parents before taking the child to the station-house.

Extracts from the Penal Law, State Labor Law and Ordinances Relative to Children.

A child under the age of seven is not capable of committing crime; a child over seven and less than twelve years of age is presumed to be incapable of crime, but the presumption may be removed by proof that he had sufficient capacity to understand the act or neglect charged against him, and to know its wrongfulness.

A person who willfully permits the life or limb of any child actually or apparently under the age of sixteen years to be endangered, or its health to be injured, or willfully causes or permits such child to be placed in such a situation, or to engage in such an occupation, that its life or limb is endangered, or its health likely to be injured, or its morals likely to be depraved, is guilty of a misdemeanor.

A person owning, leasing, managing, or controlling for himself or for another person, any of the following places, or being employed as door-keeper, ticket-seller or ticket-taker therein, who permits a child actually or apparently under sixteen years of age, to enter or remain therein unless accompanied by its parent or guardian, or suffers or permits such child to play any game of chance or skill therein, is guilty of a misdemeanor:

Dance halls, public museums, public concert saloons, public pool or billiard parlors, public bowling alleys, public skating rinks, or any place where wines, spirituous or malt liquors are sold or given away, or any theatre, kinetoscope or moving picture performance, unless such performance is given under the auspices of or for the benefit of any church, school, educational or religious institution, without profit.

Any person not being the parent, relative or friend of such child's family, who takes a child into any moving picture show, unless with the consent of the parents or proper guardian, is guilty of a misdemeanor.

Any person who permits a child to enter or remain in any house of prostitution or assignation; or

Sells or gives away or causes or permits to be sold or given away to such child, ale, wine, beer or any strong or spirituous liquor; or

Sells, pays for or furnishes to such child any cigarette, cigar or tobacco in any form; or

Being a pawnbroker or employee of a pawnbroker, makes any loan or permits to be made any loan or advance to such child; or

Being a second-hand dealer, owner, keeper or proprietor of a junk shop, junk cart, junk boat or other vehicle used for the collection of junk, receives or purchases from a child any goods, wares or merchandise; or

Sells to such child any toy or other pistol that can be loaded with powder and ball or blank cartridges; or

Employs, or causes to be employed, any child as a rope or wire walker, gymnast, wrestler, contortionist, rider or acrobat; or

Uses such child in begging or receiving or soliciting alms under any pretence or in any manner; or

Employs such child in gathering or picking rags or in peddling; or

Employs such child in any indecent or immoral exhibition, or practice; or

Exhibits such child when insane, idiotic or suffering from any unnatural deformity,

—is guilty of a misdemeanor.

Any person who employs any child for singing or dancing, or playing on a musical instrument, or in any theatrical occupation, unless such employment is as a singer or musician in a church, school or academy, or in teaching or learning the science or practice of music, or as a musician in any concert, or theatrical exhibition without the written consent of the mayor of the city, is guilty of a misdemeanor.

Make summary arrest of the person responsible for any of the foregoing violations. The child is also to be arrested and charged with Improper Guardianship.

Arrest and charge with Improper Guardianship any child actually or apparently under the age of sixteen years

Who is destitute of the means of support;

Who is abandoned or improperly exposed or neglected;

Who is in a state of want or suffering;

Who lives with a parent or guardian who has been adjudged an habitual criminal, or who has been convicted of a crime against the person of the child;

Who smokes or in any way uses any cigar or cigarette or tobacco in any form in a public place; or

Who frequents the company of thieves, prostitutes and vicious persons, or who does not subject itself to proper restraint or control by its parents, or who is between the ages of seven and fourteen years, and has sufficient bodily health to attend school and does not do so.

A parent or guardian of a child who omits to exercise reasonable diligence in preventing such child from committing juvenile delinquency or who permits such child to grow up in idleness or to commit acts which tend to injure his health and corrupt his morals, or to become a habitual truant from school is guilty of a misdemeanor. Magistrates may issue a summons for such persons.

A parent or other person charged with the care, custody, nurture or education of a child under the age of sixteen years, who wholly abandons the child in destitute circumstances, and wilfully omits to furnish necessary food, clothing or shelter for such child, is guilty of a felony.

A parent or other person who does not wholly abandon such child, but neglects or wilfully omits to provide food, clothing, shelter or medical attendance, or to make such payment toward its maintenance as may be required by a magistrate, is guilty of a misdemeanor.

No male child under 12 or female child under 16 years shall sell newspapers on the streets in cities of the first class. Boys between the ages of 12 and 14 years may do so provided they display a Board of Education badge. No child shall sell papers between 8 p. m. and 6 a. m.

No child between 14 and 16 years shall be employed without a permit from the Health Department, and when so employed shall not be allowed to work longer than fifty-four hours a week or nine hours a day, or after 10 p. m.

Handling Demented Persons.

It is generally believed, except by persons connected with institutions for the care of the insane, that a lunatic is an extremely dangerous individual, possessed of superhuman strength, and that it takes extraordinary courage and skill to manage him. Such, however, is not the case. In fact, in an asylum an attendant of average intelligence and strength usually takes care of a number of insane patients.

If your attention is called to an insane person in a public place or in some place where he cannot be properly cared for, convey him to the station-house. If he is temporarily in safe keeping, summon an ambulance and have him taken to a hospital.

If the patient is violent, try to pacify him by agreeing with him; if he claims he is the President of the United States, do not contradict him. If you are compelled to use force, use no more than is absolutely necessary. Remember that while he may have more nervous energy than a normal person, he has no more physical strength and is no more dangerous physically than the average person who resists you.

One thing to bear in mind, in this connection, however, is that you cannot subdue him by the use of tactics which depend upon the infliction of pain for results. For instance, if you bend back a normal man's finger or twist his arm, his reason will dictate submission; but an insane person, having lost, more or less, his power to reason, will not so readily submit.

Very often insane persons realize the terror their actions create and out of sheer enjoyment of their power feign to be more violent. In a case of this kind, if your manner shows that you are determined to control the patient he will generally become quiet. Do not do anything to excite his passion, but do not let him use his passion to excite you.

Be particularly cautious not to injure a lunatic. He is in reality a sick man, and it would be cowardly on the part of anyone to strike him in retaliation. If he appears to be unmanageable, get assistance, so that he may be overpowered without a struggle.

Persons suffering from acute alcoholism should be treated as insane persons, so far as placing them under restraint is concerned.

Persons suffering from hysteria are fully conscious of everything said and done in their presence. The victims are mostly nervous women. Sympathy only aggravates their condition.

If your attention is called to a case of this kind, send for an ambulance, if necessary. Pending its arrival, have the patient, if a woman, removed to some secluded place, as persons in this condition generally throw themselves about and disarrange their clothing. Speak firmly to her; tell her there is nothing the matter with her; that if she doesn't desist from further antics you will have to take severe measures to compel her to do so. In most cases, this will have the effect of bringing the patient to a normal condition.

Fugitives from Justice.

A fugitive from justice may be arrested for a crime committed in another state, if such crime were punishable as a felony in the State of New York. The courts have held that a person who commits a crime out of the state and flees into this state is not immune from arrest here.

If one person charges another with the commission of a crime in another state, which crime if committed in this state would be a felony, ask the complainant if he will make affidavit that the defendant is a fugitive from justice charged with a felony. If he assents, make the arrest. Have the complainant accompany you to make the affidavit.

Do not arrest for a misdemeanor under these circumstances without a Governor's warrant.

All cases involving correspondence or communication with authorities outside of the City of New York must be turned over to the Detective Division. If you are requested by an out-of-town peace officer to assist in making an arrest of this kind and the defendant is not actually present, refer him to the nearest station-house so that the Detective Division may handle the case.

A non-resident may be arrested in this State for a crime committed out of the State on receipt of a telegram from the authorities of the place where the crime was committed, provided a felony is charged.

CHAPTER V.

EVIDENCE, COURT PROCEDURE AND DISPOSITION OF PROPERTY.

Evidence is information which tends to refute or establish the commission of a crime or a violation of the rights of another. It may be oral, documentary or in the form of exhibits. *Oral* testimony is given by word of mouth under oath or affirmation before any court of justice or officer thereof appointed for the purpose of holding any trial, hearing, investigation, inquiry, examination or other proceeding authorized by law. The oath may be waived by consent of all parties. This is not common practice but is occasionally done when a clergyman is a witness. *Documentary* evidence consists of papers, books, etc., produced for the inspection of the court or officer presiding at any hearing or proceeding. *Exhibits* are weapons, drugs, poisons, etc., or things directly relating to the matter under investigation.

Competent evidence is evidence pertaining to the fact at issue. For instance: a statement by Black that John Smith, charged with burglary, was in front of the burglarized building at the time the burglary was committed.

Irrelevant evidence is evidence not pertaining to the facts at issue. White may testify that Smith, who is charged with burglary, looks like a man he saw assault another a year ago.

Direct evidence is testimony by which the fact at issue may be determined directly and not through inference. Greene may testify that he saw Smith force the door with a jimmy.

Corroborative evidence is that which supports and adds strength to the evidence of the main witness. Black as well as White testify that they saw Smith step from the doorway.

Cumulative evidence is evidence given by witnesses which, although not necessarily identical, is to the same effect as that given before. For instance Green testifies that he saw Smith force the door; Jones testifies that he saw him enter and White that he saw him leave the building.

Circumstantial evidence is evidence from which an inference may be drawn in regard to the facts at issue. A burglary has been committed and a quantity of overcoats stolen. Jones testifies that he saw the defendant, Smith, standing in the doorway of the building at about the time the burglary was committed; that Smith disappeared from view and, shortly after, came from the direction of the building with a quantity of overcoats over his arm.

Presumptive evidence is evidence as to facts from which the fact at issue may be presumed. If it were proven that Smith had "knockout drops" unlawfully in his possession, it would be presumed that he had the drug for the purpose of using it unlawfully.

Hearsay evidence consists of statements which the witness has heard from another person and which he repeats. It is not admissible except under the following conditions:

When the statement was originally made voluntarily by the defendant immediately after the commission of a crime;

When the statement was made in the presence of the defendant;

When a confession has been voluntarily made by the defendant. There must, however, be some other evidence that a crime has been committed. Any statement made by a defendant cannot be used against him when it is made under the influence of threats or fear, or when obtained under an official promise of immunity.

When a dying declaration has been made. It is admitted only when the person making the declaration stated that he believed that he was about to die as a result of an unlawful injury inflicted upon him.

The testimony of an accomplice is not sufficient to convict, unless corroborated by other evidence.

The testimony of a child under 12 years of age is not admissible unless in the opinion of the court such child is sufficiently intelligent to qualify as a witness. Such testimony must be corroborated.

In a criminal action, no person can be compelled to testify against himself. A prisoner is presumed to be innocent of the crime charged unless the contrary be proven.

A witness can be placed under bonds for his appearance before the proper court, and if he fails to procure such bonds, may be detained in prison.

Court Procedure.

The Criminal Courts are divided as follows:

- City Magistrates', or Police Courts;
- Special Sessions Courts;
- General Sessions Courts in New York County. (In other counties of the city, courts of similar jurisdiction are known as County Courts);
- Supreme Courts;
- Appellate Divisions of Supreme Court;
- Court of Appeals of the State of New York;
- United States Supreme Court.

Magistrates' Courts.

Magistrates' Courts have summary jurisdiction over the following cases:

- Disorderly conduct;
- Violations of corporation ordinances that are punishable criminally;
- Vagrancy;
- Intoxication;
- Violations of the Sabbath Law;
- Violations of the Highway Law, first offense;
- Cruelty to animals, in cases where defendants plead guilty.

All persons arrested for criminal offenses are arraigned in the City Magistrates' Courts. In cases over which the Magistrate has no summary jurisdiction, he holds examinations for the purpose of determining whether or not there has been established a prima-facie case (i. e. a case supported by evidence which would appear to show that a crime has been committed.) The object of this is to give the prisoner an opportunity for an immediate hearing, and to prevent the clogging of the higher courts with cases in which the evidence could not possibly secure conviction. If a prima-facie case be not established, or reasonable grounds shown to hold the defendant for a higher court, the Magistrate has power to dismiss the complaint.

A prisoner held by a magistrate on the charge of having committed a misdemeanor is sent to the Court of Special Sessions; cases of felony are sent to the Grand Jury. The Magistrate may admit to bail in either case, unless the crime charged is punishable by death.

The territory over which the Magistrates' Courts have jurisdiction is divided into districts, composed of police precincts, and prisoners must be taken before the Magistrates' Court located in the district in which the arrest was made or the offense committed. In the Borough of Manhattan, the Magistrates' Night Courts are the exception to this rule; females arrested after the closing of the day session of the Magistrates' District Courts, charged with misdemeanor, are arraigned in the Women's Night Court, and males in the Men's Night Court. Females arrested in the day time, charged with violation of the laws relative to prostitution are arraigned in the Second District Court if arrested in Manhattan, and in the First District Court if arrested in Brooklyn.

Children under the age of sixteen years are not taken to the Magistrates' Courts, but are arraigned in the Children's Court. If a child is required as a witness against an adult in a Magistrates' Court, make sure that the Society for the Prevention of Cruelty to Children is notified.

Domestic Relations Court.

This court decides all cases of abandonment and failure of husbands to provide for their families. When a warrant issued by the Domestic Relations Court is not given to a policeman to execute, the complainant is given a notice which states that a warrant has been issued and which directs any peace officer or patrolman to arrest the person named therein. In making an arrest in a case of this kind, have the complainant accompany you to the station-house.

Coroner's Court.

A coroner's court is held in each borough. Its purpose is to ascertain the cause of death of persons who have died under suspicious circumstances.

The procedure followed by policemen is similar to that followed in other courts.

Court of Special Sessions.

A Court of Special Sessions is held in each county. Three justices sit in each court, one of whom is the presiding justice. The Court of Special Sessions has summary jurisdiction over all cases of misdemeanor except libel.

Court of General Sessions, Etc.

A Grand Jury sits at designated times in each county. Its functions are to investigate all complaints charging violation of the law. As a rule, it examines only the complainant and his witnesses, although it sometimes questions the accused. If, in one of its findings, it is shown that a crime has been committed and that some individual committed it, the grand jury finds what is known as an indictment, specifying the name of the accused and the degree of crime charged, and reports to the court in which it was convened, presenting the indictment.

If indicted, a bench warrant is issued, the prisoner arrested and arraigned in court for pleading. If he pleads "guilty" to the offense charged, he is usually remanded for sentence. If he pleads "not guilty," the case is set on a calendar for trial at a specified time.

In New York County persons indicted for felonies or misdemeanors are tried by the Court of General Sessions, or by the Criminal Branch of the Supreme Court. In other counties, similar cases are tried by the County Court or the Supreme Court.

The Court of General Sessions in New York County is composed of five parts, and each is presided over by a judge, known as a Judge of the Court of General Sessions. In these courts the trials are by jury, as in county courts and supreme courts in other counties. The county courts are presided over by a county judge; and the supreme courts, by a justice of the supreme court.

Courts of Appeal.

The Appellate Division, the Court of Appeals, and the United States Supreme Courts, are courts in which appeals are made from the decisions of lower courts, and the evidence produced there is usually documentary. These courts simply pass on the legality of the action taken by the lower courts, and you will not have occasion to appear in any of them.

Court Procedure.

In criminal actions the district attorney represents the People of the State of New York in court, and it is his duty to present all the facts showing the guilt of the prisoner.

The district attorney presents his evidence first. The defendant then presents his defense, and his counsel sums up and endeavors to establish his client's innocence. The district attorney then sums up. When all the evidence in a case has been submitted, the court "charges the jury." This means that it instructs the jury on the legal rights of the prisoner and quotes the law bearing on the case.

After being charged, the jury retires. At the end of the deliberation of the jurymen, the foreman of the jury reports their verdict to the court: *Guilty* or *Not Guilty;* or, if they fail to agree, *Disagreement.*

When you bring a prisoner to court, take him to the prison known as the *Detention Pen.* After leaving your prisoner in the pen go to the complaint room and make your complaint, which must embody the facts of the violation committed by the prisoner. The complaint will be written out by the complaint clerk. If the offense charged is one in which the magistrate has no summary jurisdiction, bring the prisoner with you to the complaint room, in order that he may sign a declaration sheet and plead either guilty or not guilty. This declaration sheet is called a *formal.*

Read the complaint over carefully and see that it contains all the facts you wish made known to the magistrate. If it does not contain all these facts, call the matter to the attention of the complaint clerk and have it corrected.

A *short affidavit* is used for the purpose of bringing a prisoner's case to the attention of the court so that the magistrate may either admit the prisoner to bail or confine him to prison until the result of the examination can be determined. It charges the prisoner with suspicion of having committed some particular felony and need not embody the evidence you have regarding his case—it may simply contain the prisoner's name and address and a short description of the offense. A short affidavit can be used in a felony case only. Always consult with the district attorney or the court when drawing a short affidavit.

See to it that the complaint clerk enters the names of all the witnesses on the complaint, so that they may be served with subpoenas.

After you have signed the complaint, deliver it, with the commitment form and record card you will receive from the complaint clerk, to the attendant on the platform in front of the magistrate. When this has been done, get your prisoner and remain with him in the room adjoining the court, within call of the magistrate.

In cases where a summons has been issued or where your prisoner was bailed at the station-house, appear in court at the time specified and make your complaint in the complaint room just as though your prisoner was safely confined in the detention pen. Deliver the complaint to the attendant and wait in the court room until you hear the name of the defendant called.

If your witnesses do not appear, call the attention of the district attorney or of the court to their absence, and suggest that the case be adjourned a sufficient time to enable you to produce them. Request that subpoenas be issued for the absent witnesses.

All property required as evidence which can be conveniently brought must be in court in your custody at the time your prisoner is arraigned. If the case is adjourned, deliver the property to the Property Clerk of the Police Department. When it is next needed, you will be served with a subpoena by the proper court, and on presentation of this subpoena to the property clerk you will be given the property it calls for. Unless otherwise directed by the court, return the evidence to the Property Clerk when the case is closed.

When the case is called, take the prisoner before the magistrate and stand at the right of the defendant. You will swear that the statements contained in the complaint are true, and the complaint then becomes an affidavit. You will then be sworn by the magistrate to tell the truth in your testimony.

When you take the witness chair, sit in a position of attention; do not lounge or squirm. When addressed by the court, the district attorney, or the counsel for the defendant, face the magistrate and give your answers in a clear and distinct manner, without intention or design to influence the result. Be impersonal. You must not try to influence the court or jury by expressing your opinion. For instance, if you saw a man standing in a doorway, you must not say, "I saw him standing in the doorway and I thought he was going to break into the store," or, "I saw him running from a building and thought he might have committed a crime therein." Tell the court simply what you saw or heard and they will infer from your statements the intent of the defendant.

Do not use unnecessary words in testifying; get to the point quickly. For instance, do not say, "I went out on patrol at 8 a. m., and patrolled my post three times, and at about 10:30 a. m., while I was walking north on Broadway I saw a man passing on the east side of the street whom I afterwards learned was the defendant." Simply say, "At about 10:30 a. m. I saw the defendant passing on the east side of Broadway," and then tell everything you observed the defendant do.

In referring to a third person do not say, "this lady" or "this gentleman." If you are speaking of a prisoner say "defendant," or if you are speaking of some person or persons other than the defendant say "this man" or "this woman," or "several men and women."

The principal faults of policemen in court are:

They do not maintain an erect and soldierly appearance;

They do not sit erectly in a witness chair;

They do not speak loud enough to be heard by every person in the court room;

They show bias by trying to help the district attorney to establish the guilt of the defendant, in that they answer his questions instantly, and the questions of the defendant's counsel in an evasive manner. This very eagerness may defeat the ends of justice in two ways; an officer may give to the disinterested court the impression that he is prejudiced; or he may give a positive answer to one of the district attorney's questions in regard to time or distance, and the defendant's counsel on cross-examination may shake that testimony by proving that the officer had no means of computing the time or distance at that time.

They sometimes lose their temper and give snappy or impudent answers on cross-examination.

Do not lose your temper; answer calmly. This is most effective with the court.

Always tell the truth. Do not try to influence the court for or against the prisoner. Your power and responsibility ends when you have told the court truthfully all you know of the case. The disposition of the case is a function which is vested in the court.

The defendant's counsel will try to prove that you are mistaken in some unimportant part of your testimony, in order to establish your incredibility as a witness. If he succeeds, it will weaken the force of your entire testimony in the minds of a fair judge or jury. It will appear that if part of your testimony can be contradicted by evidence, your entire testimony could be shaken if it were possible to procure witnesses.

When you have finished giving your testimony, take your place at the right of the prisoner.

If, after the case has been disposed of by the magistrate, the prisoner is held for trial and is not bailed, you will receive from the court attendant a commitment blank, which you will deliver with the prisoner to the keeper of the prison attached to the court.

Whether the prisoner is convicted or discharged, make an immediate report to your precinct commander giving the disposition of the case and the name of the magistrate or judge presiding.

Assist and advise the district attorney or his representatives in all matters relating to criminal cases. They will send for you, from time to time, before your cases are called to trial, in order that they may familiarize themselves with the evidence and intelligently prosecute such cases.

If you are arraigning a prisoner in a magistrates' court, and are, at the time, under subpoena to attend a higher court, notify the clerk of the higher court of that fact.

When a case is held for trial, you will receive a subpoena from the court in which the prisoner is to be arraigned, specifying the time at which you are to appear. If a magistrate adjourns a case, he will direct you orally when to appear.

If you receive a subpoena from a source other than the lieutenant on desk duty in your precinct, present your subpoena to him as soon as possible, for the purpose of record. If you must appear in court during the time you would be required to be on duty according to the patrol chart, notify the lieutenant on desk duty before the beginning of that tour.

When you attend court in civilian clothes, pin your shield on your outermost garment over your left breast. Do not lounge or loiter in or about the court. Do not converse with the defendant, his counsel or witnesses. Sit in the part of the court which is specially set apart for members of the Police Department. Enter and leave court quietly. If you must leave court for any purpose before your case is called, inform the court clerk or one of the attendants of the length of time you expect to be absent and where you can be found in case your presence is required during your absence.

Do not have any conversation with a prisoner regarding counsel to be retained by him.

Disposition of Property.

The Property Clerk is the custodian of all articles recovered, or seized as evidence by the police, and all such property not held by the courts as evidence must be given into his keeping at the close of each day's session of the court.

If property is held in court as an exhibit, get a receipt from the district attorney and deliver it to the Property Clerk or inform him of any other arrangements the district attorney may make.

When property in the custody of the Property Clerk is required in court, it will be delivered to you on the presentation of your attendance subpoena. To facilitate matters, obtain the Property Clerk's voucher number from the desk lieutenant.

Property must not be delivered to claimants in court except on the order, written or oral, of the judge. In this event, obtain a receipt from the owner containing a description of the property and its value, to file with the Property Clerk.

When property is no longer required as evidence, direct the claimant to the clerk of the court to obtain a court order on the Property Clerk for its delivery. It will be necessary for you to identify the claimant before the Property Clerk.

If property is found on the street and turned over to you, give the finder a receipt and note his name and address and the circumstances. The finder becomes the lawful owner of the property if it is not claimed within six months.

Perishable property, left unclaimed on the street, is to be brought without delay to the station-house.

CHAPTER VI.

CRIMINAL IDENTIFICATION AND FINGER PRINTS.

The necessity for accurate descriptions of criminals is apparent when it is understood that of the arrests made in connection with serious crimes less than 25 per cent. are made at the time of their commission and that 75 per cent. are the result of search for criminals who get away.

For this reason, in addition to knowing the characteristics to look for in an unconscious person or dead body, every patrolman must know the points to bring out in questioning witnesses to a crime or friends of a missing person.

Above all, obtain a description that will be *individual.* An ordinary description is practically useless to the Detective Bureau in apprehending a person. Given a description calling for "a man about 30 years of age, 5 feet 10 inches, 160 pounds, dark complexion and hair, smooth face, dressed in a dark suit, black derby hat and black laced shoes," a detective might stand at Broadway and Forty-second Street and in one hour find two or three hundred men, any one of whom would answer. If we add to that description whatever distinctive personal characteristics can be discovered, such as "constant twitching of eyes," "mole (or scar) on left cheek," "finger missing," or "lower front teeth capped with gold," and "dresses shabbily," or "dresses neatly," the identification is more probable.

A general description should always contain the following items, or as many of them as can be secured:

Physical appearance: Sex, color, nationality or race, approximate age, height, weight, complexion, color of eyes, hair and moustache, apparent occupation;

Physical deformities or peculiarities: scars, moles, fingers or teeth missing, baldness, tattoo marks, nervousness or unusual habits.

Descriptions of unconscious persons, dead bodies or missing persons should contain in addition the following items:

Contents of clothing; letters, names in memorandum books or on cards, initials on handkerchief or rings, old coins, exact amount of money, watch numbers (works and case) and make;

Clothing; color and pattern of garments, name of tailor, laundry marks and initials on underwear, size and make of hat, shoes and collar.

The Portrait Parle System.

For the purpose of standardizing personal characteristics in such a manner that they may be accurately described and the description as readily understood, the Portrait Parle (speaking portrait) System has recently been brought into existence. Its practical value is so apparent that it has been almost universally adopted by the larger police departments. A little careful study and practice in watching persons passing your post will quickly familiarize you with the points to look for and the terms employed in specifying them. The following is a digest of the Portrait Parle System:

Head. In size, large, medium or small.

Profile view: straight or "gabled" (convex nose and receding forehead and chin).

Full face view: peg-top (wide forehead and narrow chin) or pyramid shaped (wide jawbones and narrow forehead).

Forehead. In size, high or low, narrow or broad.

Profile view: vertical (presenting a straight perpendicular line); projecting (further forward than the rest of face); receding (slanting back from brows); intermediate (almost vertical but receding slightly); arched or curved (presenting appearance of a bulge, almost of a quarter circle).

Eyes. The pupil is the center of the eye and is always black. The iris is the colored zone surrounding the pupil.

The iris contains two zones: the areola (next to the pupil) and the periphery. The color of these two zones generally differs but the combination gives general color of the eyes. In shape, the areola may be concentric, notched or star shaped, or radiating like the spokes of a wheel.

In color, eyes may be blue, yellow, orange, chestnut, greenish maroon, maroon or dark maroon (as in the case of a colored person).

Peculiarities of Eyes.

Twitching, caused by nervousness.
Eyes not mates in color.
Strabismus, or cross eyes.
Circle senele, or mother-of-pearl circle like the white of the eye running into the iris.
Film, or whitish skin covering the iris, similar to a cataract.
Dilated pupil, pupil naturally large or distended.
Eccentric pupil, not in center of iris.
Blindness, complete, or in one eye only; both eyes or one removed from socket.
Defective vision, necessitating eyeglasses.
Projecting, or "pop eyes," one or both, sometimes caused by disease.
Whites showing above and below iris, often an indication of insanity.

Eyelids. The opening of the eyelids governs the size of the eye, for the eyeball itself is practically the same size in every person.

The upper is termed the superior eyelid and the lower the inferior.

The superior lid may be drooping, caused by the muscles being weak, or the inferior lid may be baggy or wrinkled. Paralysis may cause one or both eyelids to droop.

If the lower lid does not cover the white of the eye to the iris, the condition is expressed by the term "raised iris."

The orbit or socket is the bony structure surrounding the globe of the eye. When the eye fills the orbit it is called full, when it sets back it is termed excavated.

Eyebrows. In size, short or long; in width, narrow or thick; bushy or scant, "pencilled" when they lie flat and are well-defined.

Eyebrows may be horizontal, arched or oblique (as in a Japanese). Brows meeting and forming an unbroken line are termed "untied," otherwise they are "tied," and in some cases the separation may be marked.

Make a note of cases in which the eyebrows differ in color from the hair.

Hair. Abundance; thick, thin, or bald (front or back, or complete).

Cut pompadour, part (position of); straight, wavy, curly, kinky (as in a negro).

Color: Blond (light, very light, medium, dark),
Red (light, medium, dark).
Chestnut, dark chestnut,
Black, jet black,
Gray, light gray,
White.

Make a note of cases in which whiskers and moustache differ from each other or from the hair.

Nose. May be termed small, medium or large. A normal nose is approximately one-third the size of the face.

The principal terms employed in describing the nose are: the root, or depression just below the forehead; the ridge; the base; the nostrils; and the partition or septum.

The ridge is classified in four ways: straight, concave, convex or humped. A concave ridge is depressed and forms what is commonly known as a "pug nose." A convex ridge is elevated and curved. When the elevation is very prominent it is termed humped. From the front, the ridge may be thin, round or flat. A flat ridge is usually the result of a fracture, and in this case the nose may deviate at the base toward the right or left.

The base is the line at the bottom of the nose. Its classifications are: horizontal (at right angles to vertical line of face), elevated (tip higher than back of nose), depressed (tip lower than back, giving the nose a long appearance).

Nostrils are classified as dilated (large or distended), pinched (very narrow), or recurrent (when a deep curve is formed on each side). Nostrils sometimes are not mates, one may be pinched or dilated and the other normal, or one nostril may be higher than the other.

The partition, or septum, is the cartilage separating the nostrils. It may be well within the nose or may extend below the nostrils.

From the front, the nose may appear narrow or wide at the bridge, and narrow, wide or flat at the base. The nose may be bell-shaped, or may be blotched, commonly referred to as a "red nose."

Lips. Dimensions: thick or thin, long or short (measuring from mucous membrane to nostrils or bottom of chin.)

The upper lip is termed the superior and the lower the inferior. Their prominence is judged from the profile. In many cases one lip projects more than the other. If the upper lip sets away from the teeth, it is called "turned up"; if the lower, "falling."

Note such peculiarities as a deep furrow running from base of nose to the tip of the lip (when scarred, usually caused by a surgical operation, termed "hare-lip"), and hair on the lip of a woman.

Mouth. In size, small, large or intermediate (measuring from corner to corner).

A pinched mouth is one that is normally tightly closed; an open mouth, one that is naturally parted, giving a gaping appearance.

The corners may be turned up or down, or the mouth may be oblique instead of horizontal.

Teeth. In size, large or small. They may be even, set closely together or slightly separated.

Note the location of missing teeth or teeth replaced by artificial ones.

Chin. In size, from the front, pointed, small, large or square. The height is measured from the opening of the mouth to the bottom of the chin.

From the profile, it may be vertical, prominent (projecting), receding or ball-shaped.

The chin may be dimpled, smooth or bi-lobed (long dimple dividing the chin into two parts).

Ear. The characteristics of the ear remain the same from birth to death. It is, therefore, a positive means of identification. In no two persons are the ears alike. At first glance they may appear similar but a little observation will reveal marked differences in shape, size, the angle at which they project from the head, or the angle they form with relation to the vertical line of the face.

In shape, the ear is generally oval, but it may be long and narrow, short and broad, square, or wide at the top and narrow at the bottom.

The border, or outer edge of the ear, may be thick or thin, narrow or wide.

The lobe is the pendulous lower part, classified as small, medium or large. The normal lobe is about one-third the length of the ear. When the front of the lobe is fastened for its entire length to the cheek it is termed blended; when it adheres only partly it is termed intermediate; and when it is totally separated it is known as a gulf lobe.

Ridges of flesh, called folds or pleats, form the inner design of the ear. When these folds or pleats project as far as the border, so that a straight edge laid across the ear would touch both folds and border, the folds are classified as intermediate; when the folds are not raised as high as the border they are classified as concave; and when, on the contrary, they are higher than the border, they are classified as convex.

The pavilion is the large hollow in the lower half of the ear. The bottom of the pavilion is termed the antitragus and it may be horizontal, oblique or intermediate. The small opening running from the pavilion toward the lobe is the intertragian canal. This canal may be absent altogether or it may be narrow or broad.

Note such peculiarities as pierced ears in a man, a lobe from which earrings have been torn leaving a slit, a pimple or island on the lobe, long stiff hair in the ear, and hematome or "cauliflower" ear.

Face. In size, large, medium or small.

In outline, pyramid, peg-top, oval, long, round or square.

Wrinkles, unless sharply defined, are not generally referred to. There are three classes of wrinkles: frontal, middle and diverse. Frontal wrinkles run all the way across the forehead and are sometimes called total wrinkles. They may be either horizontal or arched. Middle wrinkles are those which lie in the center of the forehead and do not extend the full width. Diverse wrinkles, commonly known as "crows-feet," begin at the outer corner of the eyes and extend to the temples. Horizontal or vertical wrinkles may be present between the eyebrows. A vertical furrow at this point, directly in the center is termed "middle vertical;" if to the left or right, "left vertical" or "right vertical." The grooves running from the wings of the nose to the corners of the mouth are known as the naso-labial wrinkles.

Note any one feature which may be materially larger than normal, for instance, prominent cheek bones.

Neck. In size, short or long, thick or thin.

The occipital cushion is the fatty fold at the base of the skull which, in some instances, overlaps the collar.

Look for peculiarities such as a projecting larynx (Adam's apple) and goitre.

Body. Weight and height to be approximated.

In width, gauged in proportion to the height; small, medium or large.

Note abnormal girth and defects, such as lameness, spinal curvature, one shoulder lower than the other, or shoulder blades projecting.

General attitude and habits. Some persons walk erectly and stiffly, presenting a military appearence, while others walk and stand in a careless manner, with head bent forward, backward or sidewise, or they may habitually carry their hands in their pockets, on their hips, or behind their back. Their gait may be stiff and slow, rapid with short or long steps, or measured, or swinging.

Gesticulation is very marked in some persons, often in Frenchmen, Italians and Hebrews, so much so, that many of them would have great trouble in expressing themselves if their hands were tied behind them. Gesticulation may be with the fingers, hands, arms, shoulders or head.

A person with nothing to conceal will usually look straight into another's eyes; but when the case is otherwise he will look downward or shift his eyes from right to left, unsteadily.

Seek to discover nervous habits or afflictions, such as biting of finger-nails, twitching of the features, stammering, hesitation in speaking or lisping. Note the tone of voice, whether shrill or deep, particularly a feminine voice in a man or a masculine voice in a woman.

Note the fact if the subject is a heavy drinker or smoker.

A person who smokes cigarettes habitually is likely to have his fingers stained yellow.

FINGER PRINTS.

The finger print system as a means of identification is the most positive now in use. It has been adopted by the police departments of the entire world and has proved of great assistance.

The value of the finger print system is not confined to the recording of criminals. It has been introduced into all branches of public business where positive identification is necessary. The United States Government now takes finger print impressions of all its sailors and soldiers, not only as a check on deserters, but that in time of war there need be no unidentified dead. The Municipal Civil Service Commission of the City of New York takes finger imprints of all candidates seeking positions in the Police Department at both the time of examination and appointment. The two sets of prints are then compared, so that there is a positive assurance that the person being appointed is the candidate who was examined. Savings banks use this method where the depositors are illiterate and to prevent false impersonation. By taking finger impressions of the unknown dead the Police Department of the City of New York has made numerous identifications when all other means would have failed.

The patterns of the skin ridges on the fingers are permanent, remaining unchanged through life. This has been proved by the late Sir Francis Galton, the noted scientist, who made an exhaustive study of this subject. A person's appearance may alter, he may become stout or thin, grow a beard or remove one, but the imprints made by his fingers will never differ.

The appliances required for taking finger prints are inexpensive. Ordinary white paper, printers' ink and a roller for spreading it, a slab of plate glass, and a one-inch magnifying glass commonly known as a linen tester, make a complete outfit.

Two kinds of impressions are taken, namely, rolled and plain. A rolled impression is taken by placing the bulb of the finger on a slab which has previously been thinly spread with ink, and the finger rotated from side to side, coating the ridges with ink to the very edges of the nail, then lightly rolling the finger over white paper beginning at one side of the nail and ending at the other. The imprint of each finger is taken in turn, beginning with the right thumb and ending with the left little finger. Plain impressions are taken by inking the bulbs of the four fingers and placing them simultaneously on the paper. This is done with both hands and is used to check the rolled impressions. Being taken simultaneously they must be in correct sequence and are always compared with the rolled impressions before classification. To obtain good impressions, the coating of ink on the slab should be worked out evenly and thin. The slab and ink-roller should be cleaned each day with benzine.

POLICE DEPARTMENT

CITY OF NEW YORK

F. No. F27180 B. No B34000

NAME John Brown

ALIASES "The Rat"

CLASSIFICATION No. $\frac{9 \quad U \quad 00}{5 \quad U \quad 00}$

RIGHT HAND

1—Right Thumb	2—R. Forefinger	3—R. Middle Finger	4—R. Ring Finger	5—R. Little Finger
(FOLD) \	\	\	W	W

Impressions to be so taken that the flexure of the last joint shall be immediately above the black line marked (Fold) If the impression of any digit be defective a second print may be taken in the vacant space above it.

When a finger is missing or so injured that the impression cannot be obtained, or is deformed and yields a bad print, the fact should be noted under REMARKS.

LEFT HAND

6—Left Thumb	7—L. Forefinger	8—L. Middle Finger	9—L. Ring Finger	10—L. Little Finger
(FOLD) /	/	/	/	/ (FOLD)

LEFT HAND Plain impressions of the four fingers taken simultaneously	RIGHT HAND Plain impressions of the four fingers taken simultaneously

Impressions taken by T.M.R. (Name) at Bureau of Criminal Identification,

Police Department, New York City, on March 18, 1914. 191

Impressions are divided into four types, namely: arch, loop, whorl, and composite.

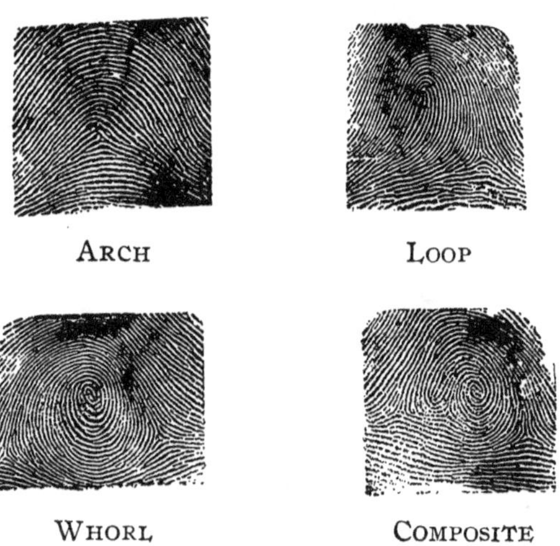

ARCH LOOP

WHORL COMPOSITE

Where large collections of finger prints are filed, it is, of course, necessary to classify them. To this end there is what is termed primary classification and secondary classification.

In the primary classification, arches are classed with loops, and composites with whorls, so that only two patterns are dealt with. The ten impressions are divided into five pairs; right thumb and right index, right middle and right ring, right little finger and left thumb, left index and left middle, and left ring and left little finger.

Of the two patterns, only the whorl is given a numerical weight, no numerical value being attached to the loop. When a whorl appears in the first pair it counts 16; in the second pair, 8; in the third pair, 4; in the fourth pair, 2; and in the fifth pair, 1.

The value of each of the first fingers of the five pairs is totaled and to this 1 is added. This gives the denominator. A total is taken of each of the second fingers of the five pairs and 1 added. This gives the numerator.

When a digit is deformed or missing so that no imprint of it can be taken, the space on the finger-print slip must remain blank. This missing finger is classified as being the same as the corresponding digit of the other hand. If the same digits of both hands are missing the impressions are held to be whorls and are classified accordingly.

Primary classifications arrange themselves from 1 upon 1 to 32 upon 32, viz.,

$\frac{1}{1}$, $\frac{2}{1}$, $\frac{3}{1}$ to $\frac{32}{1}$; $\frac{1}{2}$, $\frac{2}{2}$, $\frac{3}{2}$ to $\frac{32}{2}$, and so on up to $\frac{1}{32}$ $\frac{2}{32}$ $\frac{3}{32}$ to $\frac{32}{32}$;

making the total number of combinations obtainable 1,024, which is the square of 32.

The secondary or sub-classification is required to further identify large accumulations of primary classification numbers and is a detail which cannot be treated here. The reader is referred to "Classification and Uses of Finger Prints" published by Sir E. R. Henry, Commissioner of Police of the Metropolis, London, England.

As a detector of criminals, finger prints have often played a prominent part. Evidence of identification by means of finger prints when given by a competent witness is accepted in criminal courts.

On August 14, 1912, burglars forced porch window at residence of Charles ———, 1397 ——— Ave., Brooklyn.

On August 23, 1912, Harry ——— and another were arrested in the residence of Louis ———, at 1511 ——— Road, Brooklyn. They were brought to Detective Bureau, Brooklyn, and finger impressions taken, which were found to correspond with those on porch window.

——— was indicted by the Grand Jury, charged with Burglary—Second Offense, pleaded guilty to having entered above-mentioned porch window, and was sentenced to serve four years in Sing Sing.

FINGER PRINT EXHIBIT PREPARED

IMPRESSION OF LEFT THUMB OF HARRY ——— TAKEN AT POLICE HEADQUARTERS

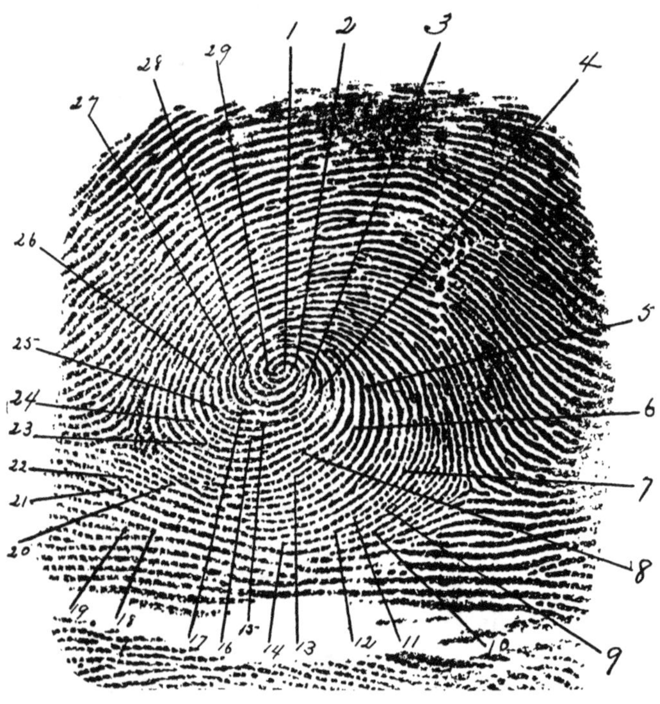

RIDGE CHAR

1 Inner Terminus
2 Ridge Bifurcates
3 Ridge Bifurcates
4 Ridge Bifurcates
5 End of Ridge
6 End of Ridge
7 Ridge Bifurcates
8 Ridge Bifurcates
9 End of Ridge
10 Ridge Bifurcates
11 End of Ridge
12 End of Ridge
13 End of Ridge
14 End of Ridge
15 Ridge Bifurcates
16 Ridge Bifurcates

A Careful Officer Preserving Finger Prints

A Careless Officer Destroying Finger Prints

FOR PRODUCTION IN COURT.

IMPRESSION TAKEN FROM PORCH WINDOW AT 1397 ——— AVENUE, BROOKLYN

ACTERISTICS

17 Ridge Bifurcates
18 End of Ridge
19 End of Ridge
20 End of Ridge
21 End of Ridge
22 End of Ridge
23 End of Ridge

24 Small Dot
25 Ridge Bifurcates
26 End of Ridge
27 End of Ridge
28 Ridge Bifurcates
29 Ridge Bifurcates

Crime investigators should know the method by which search for finger prints is made. Any article with a smooth surface, glass, metals, and highly polished surfaces, if touched, are likely to retain imprints of value. Such imprints can be developed by the aid of powders. Gray powder (mercury or chalk) is used on surfaces of a dark nature, and graphite or lamp black on white paper or surfaces of a light color. The object should be sprinkled with the powder and the powder lightly brushed off with a fine camels-hair brush. If the finger marks which appear after this process do not disclose clearly defined details they are generally useless when photographed. Care should be taken to allow nothing at the scene of a crime to be touched until a careful investigation for finger prints has been completed.

When finger prints are used as evidence in a criminal court, photographic enlargements are made of the impressions found at the scene of the crime and these compared with prints taken from the prisoner's fingers. The characteristics, such as bifurcations, abruptly ending ridges, and any noticeable peculiarities, are marked and numbered with ink. The exhibits are enlarged six diameters and a sufficient number prepared for distribution to the judge, jury and counsel. A few unmarked copies should be available in case they be required.

CHAPTER VII.

TRAFFIC AND STREET CONDITIONS.

The regulation of traffic is an important function of the Department. On account of the vast volume of merchandise and the enormous number of people in transit daily, traffic must be handled in an efficient and intelligent manner. The movement of all vehicles, both passenger and commercial, must be facilitated and permitted the greatest latitude of speed consistent with safety and convenience.

When you find traffic congested or halted, there is always a reason. You will usually find it due to a truck backed so near to an excavation or in a street so narrow that other vehicles cannot pass, or to a driver who has attempted to turn a heavy truck in the middle of the street. Congestion is often caused by a heavily laden and slowly-moving truck taking to the center of the street (particularly one with car-tracks) and retarding the lighter and faster vehicles. Do not start to move the traffic until you have found the cause of the jam. In some instances, it will suffice to straighten out the offending vehicle; in others, it will be necessary to go to the end of the block and divert the traffic coming from an opposite direction to streets less congested. Whenever possible, start the light vehicles first, for the reason that they move more quickly than the heavily laden trucks and a passageway will be quickly cleared, permitting all the vehicles to move. Try to get a passage through the center of the street first, and do not permit vehicles near the curb to move until conditions in the center of the street become normal.

After a heavy snow storm considerable congestion, which is avoidable, is found in the side streets. The Street Cleaning Department clears the principal avenues first, and the side streets sometimes contain only a passageway eight or ten feet wide. It is obviously impossible for one truck to pass another, and it is well for the man on post to keep thoughtless drivers from attempting it. Very often the start of a jam is a light wagon which has been driven into a snow-filled street to deliver some small package which could have been delivered more quickly and with less effort if the driver had left the wagon on the nearest avenue and made the balance of the trip on foot.

When regulating traffic at the intersection of streets, place yourself in such a position that you can observe vehicles coming towards you when they are a block away. When you stop north and south bound traffic to permit east and west traffic to pass, be sure to halt it at least ten feet back from the east and west crosswalks. This will give pedestrians going east and west a free and uninterrupted use of the crosswalks. The same rule applies, of course, to east and west traffic. This does away with the necessity of assisting persons, other than the infirm, across the streets.

In stopping traffic at such intersections, do not demand impossibilities of animals, drivers or operators. Your action should be governed by circumstances. Do not expect a heavily laden truck to stop as quickly as a light runabout, or vehicles on a down-grade or on slippery pavement to stop as quickly as others going up-hill over dry pavement. As you are about to stop traffic, look at the first vehicle in line. If it is a heavy truck, and from its appearance, you are led to believe it cannot stop within ten feet of the crossing without subjecting the horses to considerable effort, permit it to pass and signal the vehicle behind it to stop.

Every vehicle is required to be under perfect control of its driver or operator at all times. If it is so loaded that the horses or motive power cannot reasonably start or stop it, it is a menace to persons and property on the street and the driver should be arrested. Every person in charge of a vehicle is required to operate it at all times with due regard to the safety of persons and property, and the fact that the speed limit is not exceeded, does not excuse negligence. If the vehicle is zig-zaging from side to side, or if the driver carelessly lets go of the reins or the controlling wheel or lever of the vehicle while it is in motion, he is guilty of reckless driving and should be summoned to court; but if it appears that the act will be continued, arrest him. In presenting cases of this kind in court, base your complaint and statements upon the manner of operation and not upon the rate of speed.

When weddings, funerals, receptions, etc., are held on your post, regulate the vehicles, if necessary. If there are a great number requiring your attention for an extended period, notify the station-house and request instructions.

Vehicles are permitted to load and unload backed to the curb on certain streets, and to extend over the sidewalk if provision has been made for the free passage of pedestrians. This privilege is abused by truckmen, who back their trucks to the curb or over the sidewalk before they are ready to unload and leave them in this position after they have unloaded while they are going through a building, soliciting trade or having receipts signed. After a truck has been unloaded, the driver must turn the vehicle so that its right side is to the curb. If you warn a driver to do this and he refuses, serve him with a summons.

While the rules require that traffic must ordinarily move to the right, it is permissible to divert it to the left on occasions when by so doing better results will be obtained, as in the case of vehicles going to or coming from a theatre, reception, funeral, etc.

Heavily laden and slow vehicles must keep close to the curb; faster ones, to the center of the street. This facilitates the movement of all traffic and gives the best use of the street.

If it is necessary to speak to a driver, do so quietly. Do not threaten or yell at him. Remember that your warning or command is directed to him only, and if you can accomplish your purpose by a wave of your hand, better results follow. If it is necessary to serve a summons or make an arrest, do not stop the vehicle on a crowded thoroughfare and block traffic. Have the driver turn into a side street, where the traveling public will not be inconvenienced.

The Borough of Manhattan is twelve miles north and south and only three miles at its widest point east and west. It is therefore essential that north and south bound traffic be kept moving for the reason that vehicles from one avenue cannot be diverted into another avenue running north and south as easily as the traffic of one cross street can be diverted into another cross street running east and west. This is particularly true of the lower end of the Borough of Manhattan, where there are not more than a dozen streets running north and south. As a result of these conditions, the regulations require that wherever there is congestion, all other things being equal, north and south bound traffic shall be moved first.

Mail wagons, Fire and Police Department vehicles, ambulances, and railway and gas emergency wagons have the right of way. They must, however, be operated with regard for public safety.

When Fire Department vehicles are about to pass over your post, take your position in the center of the street, and, if necessary, divert traffic to the curb, so as to give the apparatus a clear lane in the middle of the street. Most of the accidents caused by fire apparatus happen after the first vehicle has passed, when onlookers rush out to watch where it is going and forget, in the excitement, the second and third trucks which usually follow. For this reason, keep traffic at a standstill until you are sure that the last piece of apparatus has passed and that no accidents are likely to occur.

Patrolmen on post at designated school crossings will take their position in the center of the street before the morning assembly, at noon hour, and at the closing of school, and regulate the movement of vehicles to best protect children crossing the street.

When stationed at some particular place for the purpose of keeping the public from passing, such as at a fire parade, etc., always take up your position before the crowd gathers. If you do not, it may be found that in clearing the space some person will become obstinate and compel you to use force. As a rule, the shoving and pushing is usually done by some short person in the center or rear of the crowd who is anxious to see what is going on. In a case of this kind, have someone hold your line in order that you may go to the rear and try to get the troublemaker. Persons in the front line nearly always assist in keeping the rest back for the reason that they do not want to lose their own position. Always face the crowd, so as to be in a position to instantly check any attempt at disorder, and that you may detect pickpockets working in the crowd.

PARADES AND STREET MEETINGS.

PARADES.

No procession or parade shall form or march on the streets of the City of New York to the interruption of pedestrian or vehicular traffic without first giving the Police Department thirty-six hours' notice of its object, route, and destination and obtaining a permit. The following, however, need no permits: U. S. Army, U. S. Navy, National Guard, Police and Fire Departments.

The permit issued by the Police Department to the person in charge specifies the time, date, starting point, route and destination. If you have reason to doubt that a parade passing over your post has not given the required thirty-six hours' notice, ask the person in charge, the marshal or leader, if he has a permit. If he has not, call up the station-house and find out whether a permit has been issued. In the event that it has not, place the person in charge under arrest and cause the parade to disband. In presenting a case of this kind in court, request the officer in charge of the Bureau of Information to appear for the purpose of proving that the thirty-six hours' notice was not given.

No parades or processions are permitted on Sunday except funeral and religious processions, and they may not play music or make any disturbing noise.

The following are excepted and may play music, but not within one block of a place of worship where service is then being held:

> Escorting the body in a military funeral, funeral of a United States soldier or sailor, national guardsman, veteran or member of a secret fraternal society;
>
> Military processions on Memorial Sunday to places where memorial services are held; and
>
> National Guard processions to and from places of religious worship.

If a religious procession passes over your post playing music on Sunday, warn the person in charge that he is committing a violation of law. Do not make an arrest unless you have taken every reasonable means to have the law complied with.

Street Meetings.

Persons are entitled to assemble in public places for the purpose of protesting and petitioning and, with the exception of religious meetings, require no permit. If they object to a law or rule established by those in authority, they have a perfect right to peaceably assemble for the purpose of protesting against that law or rule, as long as they advocate its change by a means prescribed by law, such as petitioning the legislature, the judiciary, or the executive heads of the city, state or national government.

They are to be afforded proper protection and are not to be interfered with *unless they attempt or threaten any act tending toward a breach of the peace or an injury to person or property, or any unlawful act.* (See Criminal Anarchy.)

While so assembled, however, they may not seriously interfere with or annoy persons residing or conducting business nearby. If complaint is made to you it will usually suffice to request the speaker or person in charge to hold the meeting at some other place where it will not be a source of annoyance.

When a meeting is held on your post and your presence may be required there for an extended period for the purpose of preserving the peace, notify the station-house so that other provisions may be made for policing the meeting.

If one of the audience annoys or interferes with the peaceful conduct of a street meeting, and the speaker requests you to do so, warn that person to cease or to leave. If he refuses to do either, place him under arrest. It is not always a good plan, after making an arrest of this kind, to leave the meeting unprotected; the ones creating the disturbance may take advantage of your departure with one of their number to break up the meeting. Summon assistance before taking your prisoner to the station-house.

PUBLIC HACKS.

A public hack is a vehicle plying for hire which solicits public patronage on the streets and highways of the City.

No hack shall ply for hire on the streets or highways without having first obtained a license from the Chief of the Department of Licenses.

The license number must be displayed on a metal plate as officially prescribed, and shall be attached to an indispensable part of the outside of the cab.

A card of the kind approved by the Department of Licenses must be displayed on the inside of the cab, bearing the license number and directing persons having cause for complaint to notify the Chief of the Department of Licenses.

If the hack is equipped with a taximeter, it shall not be operated unless the taximeter case is sealed and the gear intact. When employed, the signal on the taximeter must so indicate. After sundown the taximeter must have a suitable light shining on its face.

No person shall drive a public hack unless he is over 21 years of age and is licensed as a driver. While operating a hack, he must wear, conspicuously displayed on his coat, a metal badge containing his license number. He must also have an official card containing his license number and bearing his photograph, which he must exhibit for inspection on the demand of an inspector, policeman or passenger. No person shall drive a public hack while his license is suspended or revoked

No person shall drive a public hack without a license or while his license is suspended or revoked.

Hack drivers must not solicit passengers except while sitting on the driver's box of their vehicles, and they must not solicit passengers while the hack is standing, except at public hackstands. No other person is permitted to solicit for them.

The driver of a public hack must not seek employment by repeatedly and persistently driving to and fro in a short space before theatres, hotels, railroad stations, places of public resort, etc. He may, however, solicit employment before such places, provided he goes a distance of two blocks before turning around and repassing.

A hack driver may not carry any other than the first passenger employing him without such passenger's permission.

When a hack is hired, no person shall sit with the driver on the box.

The driver of a public hack may demand the legal fare in advance and has the right to refuse employment unless so paid.

A copy of the legal rates of fare must be posted in a conspicuous place on the inside of every cab.

When requested to do so, a hack driver shall give his passenger a receipt for the fare paid, on the official form prescribed for that purpose.

Disputes over fare are to be settled by the officer in charge of the police station nearest the scene of the dispute. Failure to abide by this decision renders the offender liable to a charge of disorderly conduct. When a dispute of this kind is brought to your attention, direct the disputants to the nearest police station. If it appears to you that a breach of the peace is likely to occur, accompany them.

At the termination of employment, the driver must search his hack for any property which may have been lost or left therein. Articles found, unless sooner claimed by the owner, must be delivered within twenty-four hours to the officer in charge of the nearest police station.

The Mayor has power to establish public hackstands at certain locations. No public hack shall stand at any public hackstand so designated, adjacent to the curb of the sidewalk within 15 feet of the entrance of any building, nor within 5 feet of any crosswalk.

Only public hacks in such number and of such kind as are designated on the metal sign post may remain at a stand while awaiting employment. When one hack leaves the line with a passenger, those behind shall move up. A public hack seeking a place at the stand shall approach the same only from the rear and shall take its place behind the last cab already in line.

Public hack drivers who violate the rules governing public hacks should be reported to the Department of Licenses and if possible the violation should be corrected. Enter in your memorandum book all the facts concerning any violation you may observe and report the same to the commanding officer of the station-house. In the following violations of the public hack ordinance, summonses should be served or arrests made:

1. Unlicensed public hacks;
2. Unlicensed public hack drivers;
3. Drivers of vehicles other than public hacks standing at designated hackstands, who refuse to move off when requested;
4. Drivers of public hacks using a license that has been suspended or revoked.

ANIMALS.

Any person who keeps or uses any place for the purpose of having any bird or animal fight, or who commits any cruelty towards an animal, is guilty of a misdemeanor.

Cruelty, under the law, means any act, omission or neglect whereby unjustifiable physical pain, suffering or death is caused or permitted.

Whenever you see a horse being driven which has sores on its neck or shoulders which the harness touches or irritates, immediately arrest the person in charge of the animal and prevent a continuance of the abuse. Have the vehicle drawn close to the curb or into a side street; remove the harness and take the horse to the station-house. Measure the size of the sore and note whether or not puss or foreign matter is in or around the wound.

The same course is to be followed in connection with a lame horse when the animal, as a result of its lameness, appears to be suffering pain while being driven.

Policemen are often called upon to destroy animals that have been injured. Do not, however, shoot an animal without the written authorization of the owner, or, if the property of a corporation, the written authorization of some person in authority, such as the superintendent, stable foreman, or the veterinary surgeon in their employ. Do not destroy an animal at the request of the driver or bystanders. It is common law and common sense that no person may be deprived of his property without due process of law, and there is no law giving you power to destroy another's property without his consent. An animal is not to be destroyed simply because it has been injured; that right belongs to the owner, and he might feel disposed to spend thousands of dollars for veterinary services to restore it to usefulness.

When a sick or injured horse has been abandoned for three hours and you are positive of that fact, you may shoot it after two citizens have examined the animal and expressed their opinion that it is injured past recovery. Enter the names and addresses of the two citizens in your memorandum book.

In shooting a horse, try first to get it close to the curb so that it will not interfere with traffic. Place the muzzle of the gun at a point four or five inches above a line drawn across the eyes and about half an inch to the left of center—that is, about half an inch above and one-quarter of an inch to the left of the point on the forehead where the hair curls. (As shown in illustration below.)

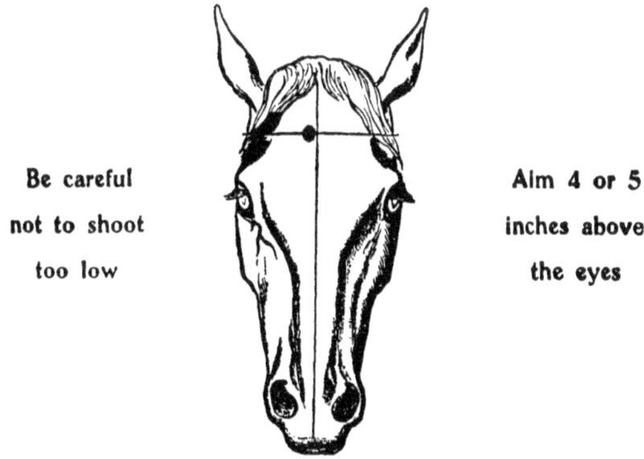

Before you fire, see that no bystander is in a position to be injured by an accidentally deflected bullet.

It is a misdemeanor to overload a horse. To determine whether or not a horse is overloaded, ask yourself: "Is this animal able to control the load it is hauling under present street conditions; can it safely stop or start the load if necessary for the protection of persons or vehicles using the streets?" If it is apparent that the horse is overloaded, place the driver under arrest, remove the vehicle to a side street, unharness the horse and have it led to the station-house.

If a horse or other large animal falls into an excavation or into the water, keep the animal from becoming excited. If possible, remove the harness with the exception of the bridle. Notify the station-house and request that the Society for the Prevention of Cruelty to Animals be notified to send an ambulance and derrick.

If your attention is called to a so-called "mad dog," confine or kill it with all possible dispatch, but be careful that you do not injure any person while shooting at it. (The following illustration shows where to shoot a dog.)

If the animal is running through the streets, whenever possible strike it on the head with your baton and stun it. If you have reason to suspect that it has bitten any person, do not destroy it if you can safely confine it, for the reason that the Health Department can more readily determine whether an animal is infected if it is alive.

If the animal is safely locked in a room when your attention is called to it, do not interfere with it. Notify the station-house so that the Health Department may send a representative to take charge of the animal.

If you are informed that an animal of a vicious nature, or one suffering from an infectious disease has bitten some person, get the name and address of the owner of the dog and of the person bitten, and notify the station-house immediately. Request the owner of the dog to tie it securely until the arrival of an officer of the Health Department. Make immediate inquiry on your post as to whether other persons or animals have been bitten. If they have, immediately notify the station-house of the names and addresses of such persons, or owners of bitten animals, for transmission to the Health Department.

No dogs shall be permitted in any public place unmuzzled.

In destroying a small animal, place it on a board, a pile of sand or some such material, so that the bullet, after passing through its body, will not ricochet and injure some bystander. The danger from a bullet deflected by a stone pavement is almost as great as from one shot directly from the pistol. (The following illustration shows where to shoot a cat or other small animals.)

Whenever your attention is called to a live or dead animal suspected of having an infectious disease, notify the station-house immediately. Guard the animal and do not permit any person or animal to touch it. If it is a horse, do not permit the harness to be removed until the arrival of representatives of the Health Department.

Dead animals in any street or place, yard, stable or building, are to be promptly reported to the station-house immediately in hot weather, at the end of the tour in cold weather.

You are required to render every lawful assistance to the Society for the Prevention of Cruelty to Animals and its representatives.

Rules for Treatment of Horses.

The following rules taken from the United States Army Drill Regulations, should be carefully observed:

Never threaten, strike or otherwise abuse a horse.

Before entering a stall, speak to the horse gently and then go in quietly.

Never take a rapid gait until the horse has been warmed up by gentle exercise.

Never ride a horse faster than a walk to the stable, or put up a horse brought to the stable heated, but throw a blanket over him and rub his legs or walk him until cool. If he is wet, put him under shelter, and wisp him against the hair until dry.

When a horse is heated, never feed grain or allow him to stand uncovered. Hay will never hurt a horse no matter how warm he may be.

Never water a horse when heated, unless the exercise or march is to be immediately resumed.

Never throw water over a horse coming in hot, not even over his legs or feet.

The saddle cloth should be placed well forward on the withers; slide the cloth once or twice from front to rear to smooth the hair. Be careful to raise the cloth in bringing it forward.

The snaffle-bit should hang so as to touch but not to draw up the corners of the mouth.

The mouthpiece of the curb-bit should rest on that part of the bars directly opposite the chin groove; the curb strap or chain will then lie in the chin groove without any tendency to mount up out of it on the sharp bones of the lower jaw. This position of the mouth-bits will be attained for the majority of horses by adjusting the cheek-straps so that the mouthpiece will be one inch above the tushes of the horse, and two inches above the corner teeth of the mare.

The throat-latch should admit four fingers between it and the throat; this prevents constriction of the wind-pipe or pressure on the large blood vessels.

Runaway Horses.

Horses run away for many reasons. High-spirited horses may break away if they are frightened by anything unusual or unexpected, such as a sight-seeing automobile, or a piece of paper blown across their path. Quieter animals, left unattended, sometimes start to walk to their stables when hungry, or seek shelter from a storm. In either case, as soon as they find they are without guidance, they break into a run. Broken harness, permitting a strap or part of the vehicle to hit the horse, is a common cause.

Runaway horses take to the part of the street least obstructed, usually the center. They will continue in a straight line unless they are in a locality familiar to them, when they will turn toward their stables or to places at which they are accustomed to stop. When badly frightened, they run blindly and do not see where they are going. In this condition, they are a serious menace to life and property.

How to Stop a Runaway Horse.

If the horse is coming toward you it is poor policy to attempt to stop him by running toward him. Nine times out of ten he will swerve from you and you will miss him entirely, or, he may suddenly swerve toward you and run you down.

Judge his speed; run in the same direction and cut diagonally across. In most cases, the horse is running blindly and will not notice you nor swerve. Then, by grasping his mane with the nearest hand and by pulling steadily on the reins with the other, he usually can be brought to a standstill.

It is very important that you keep step with the horse by running with him. That is, if you are on the near or left side, keep the left foot foremost, as if you were continually changing step as is occasionally done in marching. To a right-handed man, the left is the most natural side from which to tackle a horse, but if you try to stop a horse from the right side, reverse the process; that is, grasp his mane in your left hand, the reins in your right, and keep your right foot forward.

If both reins cannot be grasped, one rein may be pulled. Do not, however, jerk on the one rein, for by so doing there is always danger of throwing the horse, and you may be injured.

In a case where the horse has slipped his bridle, the same method may be used, except that instead of grasping the reins, clamp your hand over his nostrils and pull, endeavoring to close them entirely. This partly shuts off his wind and tends to bring his head toward his chest, in which position a horse runs only with great difficulty.

In the case of a runaway team, one of the horses may be easily mounted and in this position it is comparatively easy to control them. If you have confidence in yourself, it takes very little effort to vault to a running horse's back after once securing a grip on his mane, for the reason that the forward pull assists you into place. If you do not mount either horse, it is generally best to grasp the inside rein of the furthest horse and bring him under control

Stopping a Runaway While Mounted.

As soon as you discover that a horse is running away, prepare your horse for action by taking a firm hold on the reins and by keeping your legs close to the horse's body, so that, as the runaway draws near, you can start. Gradually increase your speed so that when the runaway draws abreast you are travelling at the same speed. Grasp the reins of the runaway horse close to the bit. Be careful to take a short hold on the reins, for if the runaway is attached to a vehicle and you take a long hold on the reins, your mount will be far to the rear of the runaway and its hind legs will be cut by the wheel or step. Horses have been so severely injured in this manner that they have had to be destroyed.

The reins should be grasped in the right hand whenever practicable. Raise the head of the runaway, in order to get better control of him. Sit well up in the saddle, pressing both knees to it, thereby increasing your purchase and preventing your being thrown if the runaway shies or stops suddenly. In this way you can gradually bring the runaway to a full stop.

The same method may be used in stopping a saddle horse. If the horse has a rider, he may be of some assistance by holding the horse to a straight course, but if the horse is riderless it is a much harder matter to stop him. Riderless, he seems to know by instinct that you are endeavoring to catch him and will wheel away as you reach; if he outdistances you he may stop, in a "come-and-get-me" attitude, and start off again as you approach. Cases of this kind have happened in parks in which there are bridle paths, where the runaway has eluded four or five mounted men for over an hour.

CHAPTER VIII.

CRIME CLASSIFICATION AND CRIMINALS.

ABANDONMENT.

A parent, guardian or legal custodian who wholly abandons a child under the age of sixteen years is guilty of a felony. To wholly abandon, in this instance, means to desert a child under circumstances in which it is not likely to receive the necessaries of life.

Failure to support a wife or child constitutes a misdemeanor.

When complaint is made to you that a parent, guardian or legal custodian fails to provide for those dependent upon him, direct that person to make complaint in the Domestic Relations Court. If the case be a felony, and if the delay necessary to obtain a warrant might defeat the ends of justice, make the arrest without a warrant. Be sure that a felony is charged.

When complaint is made to you that a child fails to provide for its parent, direct the complainant to the Domestic Relations Court.

ABORTION.

Abortion is a felony.

Section 80 of the Penal Law provides that:

"A person who, with intent thereby to procure the miscarriage of a woman, unless the same is necessary to preserve the life of a woman, or of the child with which she is pregnant, either

1. Prescribes, supplies, or administers to a woman, whether pregnant or not, or advises or causes a woman to take any medicine, drug, or substance; or,

2. Uses, or causes to be used, any instrument or other means;

Is guilty of abortion."

A reputable physician will not perform an illegal abortion, and, as a result, it is practiced by quack doctors, midwives, druggists, and in private hospitals and sanitariums. Women are usually sent to such places by the men who are responsible for their condition and who pay the expense of their treatment.

Physicians often prescribe for women who desire to avoid the annoyance and inconvenience of child-birth some harmless drug which has no effect whatever. It is mostly complaints of this kind that come to the attention of the police; for when the treatment fails the women make complaint. No arrests should be made in such cases. Convictions cannot be had unless it is proven that the operation was performed or the drug administered with intent to cause illegal abortion.

Should a patient die as the result of an illegal abortion, the crime becomes homicide.

Your attention may be called by an ambulance surgeon or by a physician to illegal abortion. Arrest the patient. Try to find out who impregnated her and who treated her. If either is present, place him under arrest and notify the station-house. Seize any evidence, such as instruments or drugs.

ADULTERY.

Adultery is a misdemeanor.

The Penal Law defines adultery as follows:

"Adultery is the sexual intercourse of two persons, either of whom is married to a third person."

In order to secure a conviction, it is necessary for the complainant to see the act of sexual intercourse committed. No conviction can be had on the uncorroborated testimony of either of the parties to the act.

CRIMINAL ANARCHY.

Section 160 of the Penal Law defines criminal anarchy as follows:

"Criminal anarchy is the doctrine that organized government should be overthrown by force or violence, or by assassination of the executive head or of any of the executive officials of government, or by any unlawful means. The advocacy of such doctrine either by word of mouth or writing is a felony."

Section 162 of the Penal Law provides that:

"Whenever two or more persons assemble for the purpose of advocating or teaching the doctrines of criminal anarchy, as defined in Section 160, such an assembly is unlawful, and every person voluntarily participating therein by his presence, aid or instigation, is guilty of a felony * * * ."

Section 163 of the Penal Law provides that:

"The owner, agent, superintendent, janitor, caretaker or occupant of any place, building or room, who wilfully and knowingly permits therein any assemblage of persons prohibited by Section 162, or who, after notification that the premises are so used permits such use to be continued, is guilty of a misdemeanor * * * ."

When you are informed that anarchists are about to hold a meeting, warn the person who owns or is in charge of the meeting place. Notify the station-house so that men may be assigned to the meeting who understand the language to be spoken.

If you are assigned to a meeting of this character, take no action unless the law is violated. Persons are entitled to assemble in public places for the purpose of protesting and petitioning. If they object to a law or rule established by those in authority they have a perfect right to peaceably assemble for the purpose of protesting against that law or rule as long as they advocate its change by a means prescribed by law, such as petitioning the legislature, the judiciary, or the executive heads of the city, state or national government, and they should be protected by the police.

ARSON.

A person who unlawfully and wilfully burns or sets fire to any building, vessel, car, vehicle, structure or other erection, is guilty of a felony.

Arson is one of the most difficult crimes in which to secure a conviction, for the reason that it must be proven that the burning was wilful, and, if the fire gets much headway, the evidence is usually destroyed.

Arson is generally committed by persons engaged in business or householders who may have met with reverses and seek, by collecting their insurance, to recoup some of their losses.

Organized bands of firebugs have come to the attention of the police. Such a band will rent a small store or flat, stock or furnish it, and after insuring it for several times its value, set it afire for the purpose of collecting the insurance.

Precaution is generally taken by such persons to start the blaze in such a manner that they may be at some distant point when the fire is discovered. A woolen cloth, saturated with linseed oil and turpentine, may be rolled and tied into a ball and thrust into a closet, to ignite later through spontaneous combustion. A more common method is to leave a lighted candle near or over some material which will ignite easily. As he is locking the place up, the proprietor casually speaks to someone so as to have a witness to the time of his departure. Knowing the length of time it will take the candle to burn low enough to start the fire, he times his return to occur after the fire has been extinguished and assumes an appearance of great concern and surprise.

If you notice a candle burning in a store under suspicious circumstances, lose no time in getting assistance and in forcing an entrance. Examine conditions in the vicinity of the candle but do not disturb anything. Notify the station-house and await the arrival of representatives of the Detective Bureau and of the Fire Department.

In addition to proving that the fire was planned, it must be proven that there actually was a fire. When a fire of incendiary origin is discovered which has not made much headway before being extinguished, permit no one to touch anything in the room until the arrival of the members of the Detective Bureau and the Fire Marshal. If but a small part of the building or property is burned or if a fire has been started in more than one spot, remove a burned part from each place in the presence of a witness, mark it for identification and have the witness do likewise. This is to prove that there was a fire. If you do not do this quickly, the firebugs may destroy all evidence of the fire. Seize anything of an inflammable nature near the scene, such as oil, saturated waste or excelsior. Do not permit anyone whom you have reason to believe is responsible for or who knows anything concerning the fire to leave the room until you have conferred with members of the Detective Bureau or representative of the Fire Department.

In sparsely populated sections of the city, barns and outhouses are burned, from time to time, by pyromaniacs, who have no other object than an insane desire to see a building burn and the fire apparatus respond to the fire.

When fires of this kind occur one after the other in a particular section, keep a close watch on those who respond each time and have no lawful reason or business there. If suspicious, question them regarding their movements before each of the fires. Look them over carefully; you may detect the odor of oil on their clothing, or, in searching them, find some inflammable material used in starting a fire.

ASSAULT.

Assault is divided into two classes: felonious assault, which is a felony; and simple assault, which is a misdemeanor.

The Penal Law defines assault as follows:

Assault in the first degree (felony).

" A person who, with an intent to kill a human being, or to commit a felony upon the person or property of the one assaulted, or of another,

1. Assaults another with a loaded fire-arm, or any other deadly weapon, or by any other means or force likely to produce death; or,

2. Administers to, or causes to be administered to or taken by another, poison, or any other destructive or noxious thing, so as to endanger the life of such other,

Is guilty of assault in the first degree."

Assault in the second degree (felony).

A person who, under circumstances not amounting to assault in the first degree,

" 1. With intent to injure, unlawfully administers to, or causes to be administered to, or taken by another, poison, or any other destructive or noxious thing, or any drug or medicine, the use of which is dangerous to life or health; or,

2. With intent thereby to enable or assist himself or any other person to commit any crime, administers to, or causes to be administered to, or taken by another, chloroform, ether, laudanum, or any other intoxicating narcotic or anesthetic agent; or,

3. Wilfully and wrongfully wounds or inflicts grievous bodily harm upon another, either with or without a weapon ; or

4. Wilfully and wrongfully assaults another by the use of a weapon, or other instrument or thing likely to produce grievous bodily harm; or,

5. Assaults another with intent to commit a felony, or to prevent or resist the execution of any lawful process or mandate of any court or officer, or the lawful apprehension or detention of himself, or of any other person ;

Is guilty of an assault in the second degree."

Assault in the third degree (misdemeanor).

"A person who commits an assault, or an assault and battery, not amounting to assault in the first or second degree, is guilty of assault in the third degree."

To strike a person with the fist, slap, shove or touch him in a hostile manner or against his will, is simple assault and is a misdemeanor. The use of a dangerous weapon of any kind constitutes felonious assault. A dangerous weapon is anything—an umbrella, cane, or bottle—which may seriously injure or cause death, if used in an assault. To inflict grievous bodily harm by any unlawful or reckless act in a brutal and inhuman manner—to severely kick a person, or to hold and punch him several times with the fist, or to throw him down and jump on him and attempt to choke him, is a felony. To aim a loaded pistol at a person with intent to shoot him is felonious assault.

When an assault is committed and a weapon used, try to secure the weapon as evidence, and mark it for identification. Have some person witness your finding the weapon and have the complainant and owner, if possible, identify it at the time.

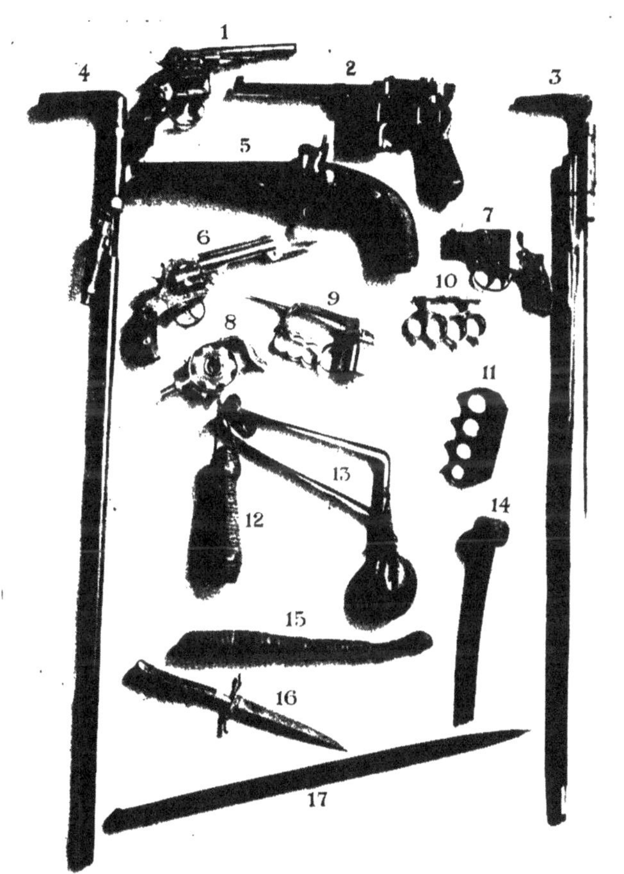

DANGEROUS WEAPONS

1 Pin Fire Revolver, foreign make
2 Magazine Pistol, "Mauser"
3 Cane Sword
4 Pistol Cane
5 Cap, Powder, and Ball, Double-barrel Pistol; very old
6 38 Caliber Revolver with Dagger
7 Vest-Pocket Pistol, 4 Barrel
8 "The Bellows" Spring Revolver, no Powder, Noiseless
9 Combination Revolver, Dirk, and Knuckles
10 Metal Knuckles, "London Dusters"
11 Metal Knuckles, "Paris Style"
12 Bludgeon
13 Sand Bag
14 Sling Shot
15 Black Jack
16 Dagger
17 Bowie Knife

Use of Force Not Unlawful in Certain Cases.

"To use or attempt, or offer to use, force or violence upon or towards the person of another, is not unlawful in the following cases:

1. When necessarily committed by a public officer in the performance of a legal duty; or by any other person assisting him or acting by his direction;

2. When necessarily committed by any person in arresting one who has committed a felony, and delivering him to a public officer competent to receive him in custody;

3. When committed either by the party about to be injured or by another person in his aid or defence, in preventing or attempting to prevent an offense against his person, or a trespass or other unlawful interference with real or personal property in his lawful possession, if the force or violence used is not more than sufficient to prevent such offense;

4. When committed by a parent or the authorized agent of any parent, or by any guardian, master or teacher, in the exercise of a lawful authority to restrain or correct his child, ward, apprentice or scholar, and the force or violence used is reasonable in manner and moderate in degree;

5. When committed by a carrier of passengers, or the authorized agents or servants of such carrier, or by any person assisting them, at their request, in expelling from a carriage, railway car, vessel or other vehicle, a passenger who refuses to obey a lawful and reasonable regulation prescribed for the conduct of passengers, if such vehicle has first been stopped and the force or violence used is not more than sufficient to expel the offending passenger, with a reasonable regard to his personal safety;

6. When committed by any person in preventing an idiot, lunatic, insane person, or other person of unsound mind, including persons temporarily or partially deprived of reason, from committing an act dangerous to himself or to another, or in enforcing such restraint as is necessary for the protection of his person or for his restoration to health, during such period only as shall be necessary to obtain legal authority for the restraint or custody of his person."

Policemen are called upon, from time to time, to eject from a car a passenger who has failed to obey some rule of the railroad company. Usually the dispute is over a transfer or the payment of a fare. Do not interfere in cases of this kind except to preserve the peace: paragraph 5 of the foregoing section empowers employees of railroad companies to use all the force necessary to make such an ejection without your help.

The ejected passenger will, almost as a matter of course, demand that you arrest the railroad employee. Inform him that you cannot interfere or arrest the employee. If he is insistent, give him your name and shield number and direct him to the office of the Inspector of the District.

"Force * * not more than sufficient to expel" does not mean that railroad employees can pummel or assault a passenger. It simply means that a passenger who is clinging to some part of a car after being ordered to get off may be forced to loosen his hold and may be pushed from the car, provided that the car is not in motion.

RAPE.

A person who perpetrates an act of sexual intercourse with a female not his wife, against her will or without her consent; or when through imbecility or other unsoundness of mind she is incapable of giving consent; or when her resistance is forcibly overcome; or when her resistance is prevented by fear of immediate bodily harm; or when her resistance is prevented by stupor produced by an intoxicating or narcotic agent; or when she is at the time unconscious of the nature of the act and this is known to the defendant ; or when she is in the custody of the law or of any officer thereof ; or when the female not his wife is under the age of 18 years, with or without her consent, is guilty of rape.

In the crime of rape, it is very difficult to obtain witnesses, and a conviction cannot be had upon the uncorroborated statement of the person raped. It is very necessary and important for the officer whose attention is called to such a crime to establish corroboration. If the crime has been committed in a building, try to find some person who saw the male and female going in or out of the building or some person who heard the girl protesting or resisting, or evidence of a struggle in the premises, such as furniture in disorder or any part of the female's clothing in the room, or her clothing torn or soiled.

If a woman complains to you that she has been raped, it is your duty to immediately arrest the man she accuses, if possible. Question the prisoner regarding his movements at the time of the alleged commission of the crime. Examine his clothing for evidence, noting if it is soiled or torn as the result of a struggle.

If the female claims she is under 18 years, secure proof of her age from the Bureau of Vital Statistics or from her baptismal record. If no force has been used, find out from her what inducement was used to make her submit.

An ambulance surgeon should be summoned to examine the victim, to ascertain whether or not a penetration had been effected recently.

Policemen on post should watch persons who are in the habit of giving unknown children money or candy, or persons who are considered degenerates or mentally unsound who give children small gifts for the purpose of gaining their friendship.

When in the vicinity of comfort stations, parks, playgrounds or schools, observe the men in and around these places who may be there attempting to entice young girls or boys for the purpose of committing rape or other unnatural crimes upon or toward them.

BIGAMY.

A person who, having a husband or wife living, marries another person, is guilty of bigamy.

Bigamy is a felony, and in order to obtain a conviction in such cases it is necessary to prove that the defendant has been married twice and that his or her lawful wife or husband is still living and has not been divorced. It must also be established that the defendant is the person named in both marriage certificates and in the record.

BEGGARS AND PANHANDLERS.

Persons wandering abroad and begging, or going from door to door, or placing themselves in the streets, highways, passages, or other public places to beg or receive alms, and children under the age of 16 years who beg or receive alms in any manner, are guilty of *vagrancy.*

Children under the age of 16 years, when arrested, are to be charged with *juvenile delinquency.*

"Panhandlers" are beggars who frequent busy thoroughfares, the vicinity of theatres, hotels, depots and similar places, and accost persons who look prosperous and kind-hearted, telling a piteous tale of lack of employment and a starving wife and family, or of coming from a nearby state or city to seek work as a mechanic and needing money to obtain a meal or lodging for the night.

If you notice one of these beggars accosting and apparently soliciting passers-by and you know that he has been previously convicted of vagrancy, arrest him and endeavor to get some of the persons solicited to appear as complainants; if they refuse, secure their names and addresses. Should his record be unknown to you, try to get some of the persons solicited to make complaint, or try to overhear the conversation that you may make an arrest. If this is not possible, ask the beggar his business and answer any question he may put as a pretext, but if you again observe him accosting persons, arrest him for disorderly conduct.

Another class of beggars go from door to door, soliciting alms, generally food and clothes, and if given an opportunity will tell a tale of misfortune and ask for money. Some of them pretend to peddle some trifling article. In cases of this kind, ask some of the householders what requests were made of them and if they reply that they were solicited for alms, arrest the beggar and take the names and addresses of the persons solicited.

Make every effort to suppress beggars of these types as they are a source of considerable annoyance to the public and often obtain alms by threatening and abusing nervous men and women. Many of them have criminal records or are criminals and if given a chance would not hesitate to commit robbery.

Most common are the beggars who place themselves in public thoroughfares wearing a cultivated woe-begone and poverty-stricken appearance. While they do not actually asks alms, they suggest it by holding out their hands or by displaying a very meager stock of shoelaces or pencils. Sometimes they pretend to be injured or deformed, or if they are injured or deformed, display their affliction in a manner intended to excite the sympathy of those charitably disposed. Arrest such offenders and charge them with vagrancy.

A trick much used by beggars is to slyly drop a crust of bread into the street and attract the attention and excite the sympathy of a passer-by by making a show of "finding" and ravenously eating it. If the ruse works and they are questioned, they have a convincing tale of starvation ready to unfold.

Sometimes a woman will be seen leading or carrying a poorly dressed and sickly looking child, and seeking alms, telling a hard-luck story of being dispossessed and of a husband out of work. She may be arrested and charged with vagrancy and with corrupting the morals of a child, in that she employed it in receiving or soliciting alms.

Professional "fit-throwers" usually work in gangs of two or three. If no policeman is in sight, one of the gang will put into his mouth a powder which the saliva will cause to effervesce, making him appear as though foaming at the mouth, and will fall to the street. As soon as a crowd collects another of the gang puts in his appearance and by questioning the "victim" brings out answers to the effect that he has a large family, has been out of work for some time, and is practically starving. The confederate then makes a little speech calling attention to "this terrible condition in a city of wealth" and when he has sympathy well aroused takes off his hat and passes it around, starting the collection by dropping into it a fair-sized bill. The contribution is dropped into the other's lap and the confederate leaves, to meet his companion at an appointed place after he "recovers" for the purpose of dividing their earnings. If you find someone ill in the street and another starting a collection for his benefit, detain them both and send for an ambulance. If the doctor pronounces the illness assumed, arrest them.

It is a felony to fraudulently obtain money under the pretext that it is for charitable purposes, and you should be vigilant in suppressing cases of this kind. If you are suspicious of persons in the garb of clergymen or Sisters of Charity who are soliciting money for some charitable purpose, question them and find out what religious community they claim to represent. Telephone and find out if they are authorized. If they are not, arrest them and get as many persons as you can who have been duped, to appear against them.

BLACKMAIL AND EXTORTION.

There are organized bands of blackmailers who terrorize business men and shopkeepers by demanding large sums of money and threatening to do some injury to them, their property, or family, in case they are refused.

The victim is usually directed to leave the money at some place where one of the gang will call for it, and is warned that if he refuses or notifies the police, his house will be blown up, his children kidnapped, or his horses poisoned.

A great many persons submit to this form of extortion, especially when their children are in danger. The principal sufferers are foreigners who are not familiar with the English language or customs.

Similar methods are also used by unscrupulous merchants to drive competitors from the vicinity of their stores. They usually warn their competitors to move, and if they refuse, hire bomb-throwers to place explosives near the places of business, to scare them.

The material used in the manufacture of such bombs is generally stolen from contractors who make use of explosives, by the laborers employed on their work. The fuse ordinarily used ignites and burns quickly. To give them more time to escape after lighting the fuse, the bomb-throwers attach a wax taper or piece of hemp cord to the regular quick fuse. This allows them five or ten minutes in which to get to a safe point.

The bomb is placed in the doorway or hall of the building selected, often being carried there under the bomb-thrower's coat. He then lights a cigar or cigarette, and at the same time ignites the wax taper or the hemp cord. They sometimes light the regular quick fuse from the cigar or cigarette they are carrying, while passing in front of the building, and then toss the bomb into the hall.

Upon investigating an affair of this kind, it will be found that the person threatened is generally reticent. He will shake his shoulders, bite his finger-nails, refuse to give any information, and deny that he ever received threatening letters. He may threaten to "get even" in his own way.

It is difficult for the man on post to arrest the person who has placed an explosive, unless he sees him at or near the scene of the crime or has received information from other persons who saw the explosive placed, for the reason that sufficient time elapses before the explosion to enable the guilty one to go a considerable distance from the scene.

Secure whatever evidence you can, such as matches and fragments of the bomb near the scene.

Horse poisoners usually enter a stable by force and mix the poison in the grain in the feed-bins, or place an apple, the core of which has been removed, filled with poison and plugged, in the manger. They will also follow a team and when the horses are eating on the street and the driver is out of the way, either drop the poison into the feed-bag or give the animal a poisoned apple. Sometimes these gangs employ children to feed the poisonous substance to the animals on the street.

If you find persons in or around a stable under suspicious circumstances, in addition to finding out whether or not that person has a lawful reason for being there, cause an investigation to be made immediately of the mangers and feed-boxes to ascertain whether or not they contain any poisonous matter. Be suspicious of any person tampering with feed-bags, whether the bag is on the horse or in the wagon, and of persons who feed apples or sugar to horses on the street. It is a felony to poison horses or to allow any poisonous matter to be near or around them with the intent that it be eaten by them.

Blackmail and extortion are similar and it is sometimes difficult for a patrolman to distinguish between the two. It is a safe rule to follow, however, that where a threat, oral or written, has been made to do an injury to a person, his family or property unless money or other consideration is forthcoming, the person or persons participating in said threat, who receive any consideration as a result, have committed a felony and should be arrested.

As a class, the persons who commit such crimes are idlers, with no visible means of support, and their reputation is known to a great many of their own race. They congregate in wine rooms, saloons, lunch rooms and coffee cafes where cards are played.

You can be of invaluable assistance to the Detective Bureau by ferreting out evidence and communicating whatever you find to your commanding officer or to the members of the Detective Bureau. If you gain the confidence of the reputable business people on your post and if they feel that they can depend upon you not to reveal their identity, they will give you information regarding the operation of those of their own race who are engaged in this nefarious business.

Extortion, in another form, is practiced by dishonest public officers, who permit persons to violate the law for a consideration, and use their office as a means of intimidating them. A public officer, or a person pretending to be such, who unlawfully and maliciously, under pretense or color of official right, arrests another or detains him against his will, or who seizes or levies upon or dispossesses another from his property, or does any other act whereby another person is injured in his person, property or rights, commits oppression and is guilty of a misdemeanor.

A police officer who makes an unlawful arrest or levies upon another person's property, except as provided by law, in addition to being punished criminally, is liable to damages for the injury the person has sustained as a result of his unlawful act.

BRIBERY.

The Penal Law defines bribery as follows:

"SECTION 371. *Bribery of a judicial officer.* A person who gives or offers, or causes to be given or offered, a bribe, or any money, property, or value of any kind, or any promise or agreement therefor, to a judicial officer, juror, referee, arbitrator, appraiser or assessor, or other person authorized by law to hear or determine any question, matter, cause, proceeding, or controversy, with intent to influence his action, vote, opinion, or decision thereupon * * * (is guilty of a felony). * * *"

"SECTION 372. *Officer accepting bribe.* A judicial officer, a person who executes any of the functions of a public officer, * * * who asks, receives, or agrees to receive a bribe, or any money, property, or value of any kind, or any promise or agreement therefor, upon any agreement or understanding that his vote, opinion, judgment, action, decision, or other official proceeding, shall be influenced thereby, or that he will do or omit any act or proceeding, or in any way neglect or violate any official duty * * * (is guilty of a felony). * * *"

"SECTION 379. *Bribery of witnesses.* A person who is, or is about to be, a witness upon a trial, hearing or other proceeding, before any court or any officer authorized to hear evidence or take testimony, who receives, or agrees, or offers to receive, a bribe, upon any agreement or understanding that his testimony shall be influenced thereby, or that he will absent himself from the trial, hearing or other proceeding, is guilty of a felony."

In making arrests under this law, whenever possible do so under the advice and direction of a superior officer. It is necessary to have the money, or other consideration used, marked. The marking should be done in the presence of witnesses and a memorandum made of the mark used. There should always be a witness to the passing of the bribe and before the consideration is turned over, the receiver should be questioned fully as to what is to be expected from him in return, that there may be no doubt as to the object of the bribe. If he puts the bribe on his person, note where he puts it and as soon as he is arrested have him searched, in the presence of the witness who heard the conversation. Do not permit the accused to get out of your sight from the time the bribe is handed to him until he is arrested and searched. When the money or other consideration is recovered, set it aside carefully as evidence.

DISORDERLY CONDUCT.

Any person who shall, by any offensive or disorderly act or language, annoy or interfere with any person in any place or with the passengers of any public stage, railroad car, ferry, or other public conveyance, or who shall disturb or offend the occupants of such stage, car, ferry or conveyance by any disorderly act, language or display, although such act, conduct or display may not amount to assault or battery, shall be deemed guilty of a misdemeanor.

Section 1458 of the Consolidation Act, in effect:

"Every person in said city and county shall be deemed guilty of disorderly conduct that tends to a breach of the peace, who shall in any thoroughfare or public place in said city and county commit any of the following offenses, that is to say:

1. Every person who shall suffer to be at large any unmuzzled ferocious or vicious dog.

2. Every common prostitute or nightwalker loitering or being in any thoroughfare or public place for the purpose of prostitution or solicitation, to the annoyance of the inhabitants or passers-by.

3. Every person who shall use any threatening, abusive or insulting behavior with intent to provoke a breach of the peace or whereby a breach of the peace may be occasioned."

To constitute disorderly conduct, some physical act must be committed, such as to unnecessarily yell, shove, push or jostle, or to block or impede pedestrian or vehicular traffic on the streets.

Do not confuse "disorderly conduct" with "disorderly person." A disorderly person can be arrested only on a warrant. The difference is that in disorderly conduct an *overt act* must be committed, while in the case of a disorderly person, such as a man who fails to provide for his family, a fortune-teller, an habitual criminal, etc., no overt act or breach of the peace is committed or threatened.

To threaten a breach of the peace, as specified by the provisions of the Penal Law, means to commit any act which is likely to cause a breach of the peace, such as one person inviting another to fight or verbally threatening to injure him or his property.

You will find the chief offenders young men who may be employed at some legitimate trade but who congregate in the evening on the streets and corners and take delight in insulting and annoying aged persons and young women, and youths "shooting craps" on the street, blocking the sidewalk and annoying and interfering with passing pedestrians. While a woman who is insulted by these rowdies will complain to the patrolman on post, she usually refrains from appearing in court.

When you find young men congregating and showing tendencies toward becoming disorderly, warn them. If that does not suffice and they actually become disorderly, arrest them and try to get witnesses or complainants to appear in court to corroborate you.

"Car rowdies" are a source of considerable trouble in the summer time. Very often a number of men after having attended some function or visited a pleasure resort return home in high spirits and take possession of a car. The guard or a civilian may command them to stop their antics and in this way start a fight. If your attention is called to a condition of this sort and you cannot cope with the crowd single-handed, request someone to have the operator signal for assistance, and if on a subway or elevated train signal and hold the train at the next station. While waiting for assistance, get some person in the car to guard the door to prevent the escape of any of the participants, then single out the leader of the mob and place him under restraint. As a rule his friends will soon become submissive. Upon the arrival of assistance point out each person whom you saw or heard commit any act of disorder and cause his arrest. Make a note of the names, addresses and badge numbers of the railroad employees and the names and addresses of the persons who were annoyed or who witnessed the affair, and request them to appear in the proper court at the time of arraignment.

To convict under disorderly conduct, it is necessary to prove that the individual arrested committed some overt act; therefore, when your attention is called to a disorderly crowd, try to remember the particular act committed by each person, that you may present the complaint intelligently in court.

When pickpockets are found in a conveyance or in a crowd in the street, shoving, jostling or annoying persons, they should be arrested and charged with disorderly conduct. At the time the arrest is made, persons in the conveyance or crowd should be requested to examine their clothing to see if anything has been stolen from them. In this way you may get a complainant to charge them with larceny.

HOMICIDE AND SUICIDE.

"Homicide is the killing of one human being by the act, procurement or omission of another."

To kill "by the *act*" means to assault—to shoot or to stab.

To kill "by *procurement*" means to cause one person to kill another.

To kill "by *omission*" means to fail to provide ordinary measures for the safety of others, e. g. when a contractor fails to provide planking on each floor of a building in course of construction, and as a result, a workman falls between the beams and is killed.

Homicide is divided into four classes: Murder, manslaughter, justifiable homicide, and excusable homicide. Each class is a felony; that is sufficient for all police purposes—do not attempt to determine the class or degree of a homicide; that is the function of the judiciary.

Make summary arrest in all homicide cases except when the victim is killed by a railroad engine, car, truck, or the like, and you find, on investigation, that death was caused purely through accident. If in doubt, present the facts to a magistrate and apply for a warrant.

In homicide cases it is absolutely essential that a proper identification of the body be made to the Coroner's Physician before the autopsy is performed. To this end, the following steps must be taken in order to establish the *Corpus Delicti.*

The first member of the force to arrive at the scene of a homicide must identify the body of the deceased to the Coroner's Physician at the inquest as being the body of the person he found at the scene of the homicide.

The same officer must procure the attendance at the inquest of one or more persons, relatives of the deceased if possible, to identify the body in the presence of the Coroner's Physician as the body of the person whom they knew during life. The officer should make a memorandum of this identification for future use.

In a homicide case, as a means for future identification, attach a tag bearing the date and the names of the deceased and defendant, to each article of clothing worn by the deceased at the time of the attack, and mark it for identification in the presence of witnesses. The clothes, if powder scorched, may prove that the assailant stood close to the victim, or they may prove that the bullet came from a certain direction. The clothing, in addition, may enable persons who had not seen the face of the victim in life, but who had noted the color or design of the clothes, at the time of assault or immediately after to identify him. In addition any weapon that may be found and every object that may be used later in connection with the case should be similarly marked. Where the victim of an attack is dying or is seriously injured, the same precautions should be taken.

When a pistol which has been used in the commission of a crime comes into your possession, unload it, carefully mark the weapon and the loaded and discharged cartridges for identification with a scratch, and have a witness to such marking. Note the manufacturer's name and the calibre and serial number of the pistol, and numbers and letters on cartridges.

Keep weapons in the same condition as they are found; blood should not be removed from a knife, nor rust from a revolver.

Look for anything that may be considered as evidence, such as burns on the hands, powder marks, empty shells, etc. If an automatic pistol has been used, the empty shells will be found about ten or fifteen feet to the right and a little to the rear of the place from which the shot was fired, for the reason that the shells, as they are automatically ejected, are thrown in that direction. The smell of burned powder often clings to a person's pistol hand for quite some time after a shot has been fired, even though the pistol was thrown away immediately after.

Do not let evidence get out of your sight or control until you have marked it. Deliver the evidence in person to the Property Clerk.

When investigating a case which may become one of homicide, make every effort to obtain from the injured or dying person his ante-mortem statement. Such statements are of the greatest importance to the public prosecutor, and without them convictions could not have been obtained in many cases.

The principal element to be considered in taking a dying declaration is the mental attitude of the person making the declaration. In order that his statements may be admissible in evidence, he must have no hope for recovery at the time. It is to this fact that special attention is called. The patient should be fully interrogated on that point before a statement is taken. Ask the attending physician the condition of the victim. If he states that the injured person is likely to die as a result of the injuries request him to inform the patient of his profession and of that fact.

In all cases the dying person should be questioned as follows:

Question: What is your name?
Answer:
Question: Where do you live?
Answer:
Question: Do you believe that you are about to die from the effects of the injury you have received?
Answer:
Question: Are you willing to make a true statement of how and in what manner you received the injury from which you are now suffering?
Answer:
Statement:

There should be at least two witnesses to a dying declaration, one of whom should be the attending physician.

If possible, reduce the questions and answers and the statement to writing and have the victim sign it after he has heard it read. Also obtain the signatures of the witnesses to the declaration.

On arriving at the scene of a homicide or an attempted homicide, summon medical aid at once. If you are within a building, this can be done without leaving the room, by blowing your whistle or calling from a window and requesting any person to notify police headquarters to send an ambulance and detectives to the premises.

If the ambulance surgeon pronounces the victim dead, under no circumstances permit removal of the body without the authorization of the Coroner or the commanding officer of the precinct. If the body is in a street or other public place, cover it with a sheet or something similar, which may be obtained from a nearby storekeeper or resident. If the body is in the center of the street or sidewalk and interferes with traffic, remove it to the curb or into the house line.

In cases of suicide or attempted suicide, secure the weapon or poison used. Place under arrest all persons who attempt suicide and remain with them until you are properly relieved. Do not be too quick to conclude that the case is one of suicide; a clever murderer may have arranged a suicide scene.

Keep cool. Remember that you are there for three specific purposes: First, to arrest the perpetrator; second, to get evidence; third, to get witnesses. If you do these three things as well as you can the case will usually be cleared up. If you do not, it will be incomplete and other members of the Department will have to go over the ground again.

Policemen are often justly criticized for the incomplete manner in which they present homicide cases in court. This failure is due mainly to their having been excited at the scene of the crime and having failed to observe conditions. Neither the court, jury, nor district attorney has witnessed the scene, but you have; and it is reasonable for them to expect you to paint a verbal picture of the surroundings with especial regard to distance and relative position of nearby things to the body, such as doors and windows, furniture, the curb, doorways, street-lamps, letter-boxes, and the weapon, so that from your testimony they may almost imagine that they are viewing the situation as you found it. You are called upon to use your power of observation in a homicide case more than when investigating any other class of crime, because the victim, who would ordinarily be the complaining witness, is dead, and unless there is an eye-witness to the crime, you will have to infer from the circumstances what actually happened. Use your brain and imagination. Ask yourself: "How was this crime committed?" "Why was it committed?" "What was the motive, revenge or jealousy?" "Was it done in the sudden heat of passion?" or "Was it done with intent to commit some other crime?"

If the homicide has been committed in a room, permit no unauthorized person to leave or to enter until the arrival of members of the Detective Bureau, the District Attorney's Office, or the Coroner. Establish the identity of each person before he is permitted to leave, and make each one show you proof that he is the person he claims to be.

Permit no one to touch or handle any weapon or furniture which might contain finger impressions of the assailant. If there is evidence of a struggle, such as furniture or bedding disturbed or blood-stained, do not disturb it.

Do not talk unnecessarily. Pay careful attention to what persons within the room or bystanders have to say; in this way you may get some important witnesses. If you are suspicious of any person, or if you have reason to suspect why or by whom the crime was committed, tell your suspicions to members of the Detective Bureau, to the District Attorney, and to the Coroner. Tell nothing to bystanders or to your friends.

If you are suspicious of any person, but are not justified in making an arrest, do not let that person know of your suspicions by your actions. If you make an arrest, do not let your prisoner or his friends know what you know about the case. Try to find out what they know. Question your prisoner immediately after placing him under arrest and note the questions and answers in your memorandum book. *A statement made by a prisoner immediately after his arrest is admissible in court.*

Assist the members of the Detective Bureau, the District Attorney, and the Coroner in every way. Answer their questions and volunteer all the information you may have about the case.

If you are assigned to work on a homicide case, do not get disheartened if you follow a clue and it does not prove right. Take up another, and keep at it. Remember that there is a right clue to every homicide, and that if you find and follow the right one it will lead to successful results. Every unsolved murder has remained so because the members of the Department failed to find the right clue.

INTOXICATION IN A PUBLIC PLACE.

Public intoxication is a misdemeanor.

In order to justify arrest, however, the person must be helpless or without the use of his faculties in a public place, and a menace to himself or offensive to public decency.

If a person is partly intoxicated but is able to walk without annoying or interfering with others in their right to the use of the street, there is no violation; but if, as a result of his being partly intoxicated, he jostles or interferes with others, arrest him on a charge of intoxication.

You may not arrest a man for intoxication in his residence: it is not a public place.

Persons partly intoxicated, singing or shouting as they pass through a residential section at night and interfering with the repose of the neighborhood, should be promptly warned to stop it. If they persist they should be arrested and charged with disorderly conduct.

MALICIOUS MISCHIEF.

A person who unlawfully and wilfully injures any real or personal property of another without his consent is guilty of malicious mischief and is punishable according to the value of the property destroyed. If the value of the property destroyed or the dimunition in the value of the property caused by the injury is less than $50, it is a misdemeanor; if over $50, it is a felony. It is a felony to interfere with the operation of a railroad train by placing any obstruction on the track or by tampering with any signal, brake or coupling. It is also a felony to unlawfully break or deface any part of a house of worship or any of the property therein.

The principal crimes under malicious mischief with which the police have to do are the breaking of windows, the defacing of fences, trees and shrubbery, and the sending of false alarms of fire.

When making arrests for malicious mischief, have the complainant appear in court to prove that the property was destroyed without his consent.

LARCENY.

Any person who, with intent to deprive or defraud the true owner of his property or the use and benefit thereof, steals such property or appropriates the same for his own use or that of any other person, by fraud, cheat, misrepresentation, trick or device, is guilty of larceny.

Larceny is divided into two classes, grand and petit. Briefly defined, grand larceny is a felony and is the theft of any property from the person, or of property exceeding Fifty Dollars in value; petit larceny is a misdemeanor and is the theft of property not exceeding Fifty Dollars in value and not from the person.

A person who takes or uses an automobile or motor-vehicle without the consent of the owner is guilty of grand larceny.

One who finds lost property under circumstances which give him knowledge or means of inquiry as to who is lawfully entitled to it and who fails to make every reasonable effort to find the owner and restore the property to him, is guilty of larceny.

Any person who brings into this state any stolen property is guilty of larceny.

BURGLARY.

Burglary is the unlawful entry of a building with intent to commit a crime; by breaking into it, through collusion with some person already in, or by deceiving an occupant or other person as to the motive for entering.

To convict in a case of burglary it is necessary to prove three elements:

First: *Intent to commit a crime.* This is usually inferred from whatever the prisoner has done in the building; or, if he has not succeeded in stealing anything, from the suspicious circumstances of his being in or about that particular place without a legitimate reason.

Second: *Entry.* This means the entry of any part of the burglar's body into a building, or of any tool, weapon or instrument in his hand. If he puts his finger tips or his head into a building, the entry is just as complete as though he went inside and remained there for hours.

Third: *Manner of entry:* by *breaking* in, through *collusion* with someone within, or by means of *subterfuge.* To *break* in means to force open any aperture, such as a door or window. If a door is unlocked or partly open and it is necessary for a person to force it in order to permit his body to enter, the break is just as complete as though he used a crowbar and tore out the side of the building. Through *collusion* means, for instance, the admission of a thief by a servant or other employee who is aware of his intention to burglarize the house. The person so aiding is a principal and is also guilty of burglary. By *subterfuge* means entry gained under some pretext, such as a thief representing himself to a servant as a gas inspector or mechanic.

NOTE THE DIFFERENCE A

CHANGE OF CLOTHES WILL MAKE.

The term "building," used in this sense, means any store, house, boat, railway car, shanty—in fact, anything with a roof and four sides.

Assuming that a man breaks and enters a building with intent to commit a crime, the moment he enters he has committed burglary. He is punishable separately for each crime he commits in the premises; for instance, if he steals an article of value he may be charged with larceny, if he strikes a person he may be charged with assault, or if he destroys property he may be charged with malicious mischief.

Practically every burglary is prearranged and the details planned. Burglars naturally guard against the ordinary precautions which they think a *live* policeman will take to prevent the crime or to capture them, so in order to be successful in preventing burglaries on your post, you will have to put more than ordinary effort into your work. Do not imagine that every burglar or thief wears a peak cap, box coat, sweater, striped pants or bull-nosed shoes, so typical of stage burglars. They realize that to dress in such a manner would arouse immediate suspicion and, accordingly, dress and carry themselves in a manner least likely to attract attention. They do not, as most persons believe, carry burglars' tools on their person at all times. They know that it is not only a violation of the law but that it is circumstantial evidence as well, and consequently carry tools no longer than is absolutely necessary. Sometimes, they hide the tools near the scene of the intended burglary. If they have tools in their possession and think they are going to be searched, they will try to hide them or throw them away. Tools are carried frequently in musical instrument cases. (See illustrations on pages 132 and 133.)

In making arrests in connection with burglary be careful to observe and note all the conditions under which the crime was committed, such as the manner of entry, the particular part of the building forced, whether in the day or night time, whether or not the premises were inhabited, whether any person was assaulted, and whether or not confederates assisted. It is necessary for the District Attorney to know each element so that he may intelligently present the case to the Grand Jury, and that they may know the particular degree of crime that has been committed.

When you have anything to do with burglars, take no chances with them. Remember that some of them would kill you if, by so doing, they thought they could escape.

Dutch House Men.

There are many different types of burglars, who resort to various means in plying their calling. The burglars most dangerous to society are those known as "Dutch house men." They are the most desperate. They always work heavily armed and to accomplish their purpose or to avoid capture will take life under the slightest provocation. They usually operate in an inhabited dwelling, and to gain entrance, secrete themselves in some part of the building or grounds until they think the occupants have retired; then, if necessary, they make their way to a roof, fire-escape or porch, and get in by prying open a skylight or jimmying a window sash.

As a rule, householders fasten windows leading to fire-escapes or porches but are careless about the other windows. "Dutch house men" know this failing and often take advantage of it. They fasten one end of a rope (which one of them may have carried wound around his body) to a chimney on the roof and drop the other end over the ledge. One of them will lower himself to the desired window, open it and enter. They generally seek the place where it is most likely that valuables have been left before the owner retired, such as the tops of dressers or the pockets of clothing. In going from room to room, they usually place some obstruction, a table or a chair, in such a position that if the occupant should awaken and attempt to leave the room he would trip over the object and make

BURGLAR WORKING WITH ROPE.

enough noise to warn the burglar that his presence had become known. Unless they are sure that no alarm has been given, they will seldom leave by way of the street; usually they secrete themselves on the roof or in the back yard and remain until there is an opportunity to escape. (See illustration on page 136.)

When your attention is called to burglars of this kind, try to get assistance. It is not well to rap your baton or to make a noise in getting assistance in these cases; try to send a messenger. If there is a burglar in the premises in question, being of a cautious nature, he will be listening for any sound and can judge from any noise you make your exact location, whereas you do not know where he is. Have your pistol drawn, ready for instant use. Surround the building, if possible, before entering and guard the room. When the place is securely guarded make a systematic search of every part of the building and the surrounding grounds; examine chimney flues, dumbwaiters, shafts, barrels, areaways, and the inside and top of water tanks on the roof. Burglars have been known to hide in these places until the police have given up the search, and then escape.

Flat Thieves.

Flat thieves are not as desperate, but manage to steal considerable property. As a rule, they will not enter an apartment while anyone is at home. They profit by the knowledge that housekeepers generally hide their money and valuables in a nook where they think a thief will be least likely to look, under rugs, legs of tables, between mattresses and beds, in sewing-machine drawers, etc.

A flat thief requires only about five minutes in an ordinary flat, and when he is through it looks as though an earthquake had shaken the building. He starts by pushing the furniture to one end of the room; he turns the rugs over, empties the contents of bureau drawers into the middle of the floor, where they are examined, throws mattresses to the floor, cuts them open if he has not already discovered the hiding place, turns vases and bric-a-brac upside down, and, in this way, has every part of the flat searched in a very short time.

Flat thieves are usually young men between the ages of sixteen and thirty years. They gain entrance by ringing the vestibule bells and, if no response is made, they assume that no one is at home, and enter the hallway and proceed to the apartment selected. If the door is locked, they either use a false key or jimmy it open. Or, they may watch persons leaving their apartment, and enter during their short absence. If questioned, they try to represent themselves as peddlers, agents, inspectors of telephone, gas, water or electricity, or mechanics. They usually bundle together the proceeds of a theft and carry it to the street, passing through the halls with an air of bravado, so as not to excite suspicion. They generally work in pairs; one standing in the hallway to warn his partner of the return of the tenant, and, in case the thief is pursued, to trip the person in pursuit or to divert him in some other way. They seldom leave a house together, but usually meet at a distance from the scene to dispose of the property and divide the proceeds.

Patrolmen should particularly observe men coming from flat-houses or private residences in the afternoon as well as at night, with bundles, or men who look suspicious. If you notice someone with a bundle and are suspicious, stand in a position as though you were about to stop him. A thief will usually become scared and show evidence of fear. If he does, grab him. Have him explain his movements and expose the contents of the bundle. Look for some distinctive mark, such as the monogram or maker's name on jewelry, or the tailor's name or color of lining in clothing, and question him along that line. If he has stolen the stuff, he will probably not be able to answer you correctly; this class of thieves must work so quickly that they have not the opportunity to familiarize themselves with such data.

When you question suspects concerning their occupation, check up their answers by their physical appearance or manner of dress. If a man is engaged at some laborious vocation his hands or clothing will show evidence of it; if he is engaged in a clerical capacity you should see proof of it. Smart thieves anticipate being asked such questions if they are stopped and dress so as to conform to the appearance of persons following the vocation they intend to name.

Many flat thieves work by hiring a room or flat in a residential section of the city and as near the roof as possible, particularly where the roofs in the vicinity are of about the same height. They use scuttles and fire escapes as a means of getting into buildings, and convey their plunder over the roofs to their rooms. In this way they avoid the danger of being detected on the street.

To get their plunder to a receiver, however, they must take it to the street. Be suspicious of persons whom you see frequently taking a bundle or suit-case to or from a residence. Even though you find they reside there, make discreet inquiry as to their employment.

Loft Burglars.

Loft burglars are the most feared by merchants, for when they make a haul, it is usually a big one, amounting to thousands of dollars. They are necessarily the brainiest of burglars for the reason that their work requires more and better planning. Usually, they travel in gangs of from three to six, and always go prepared with tools to chop through any part of a building. Plans are often made weeks in advance. A loft is selected after a study of its location and the quantity and quality of the stock carried in it. Weeks are then spent in becoming familiar with the habits of persons who might be in a position to thwart or discover them, particularly the watchmen and patrolmen on post, and the customary time of opening and closing the building, noting the person to whom this duty is entrusted.

A Saturday afternoon or night is generally selected for the entry. Sometimes it is necessary to gain entrance through a building three or four doors away and clamber back over the roofs. When the loft selected is reached they do not hesitate to cut through a wall to get one of their number into it; if necessary, they will drill through the floor from the loft below or through the ceiling from the one above, lowering the first man down with a rope. The door of the loft is then opened from the inside if the circumstances warrant it.

The loot is carefully selected from the most valuable stock. Packing cases are constructed from material lying about, filled, and nailed shut.

They are now confronted with the most difficult task, that of getting the packing cases from the building. The property is seldom moved at night. They fear that the appearance of a vehicle at an unusual hour in a section of the city where lofts are located would arouse suspicion. Instead, if, as a result of their previous study, they know that the loft will be opened at 7:30 a. m., a vehicle will be brought to the front of the building at about 7:20 a. m., the door opened from the inside by one of the gang dressed as a porter, and in the most bold and daring manner the cases will be loaded on the wagon. One of the gang may even engage the patrolman on post in conversation, possibly within sight of their activities. The bogus porters, if the circumstances necessitate it, will go back into the building and escape by way of the roof or through an adjoining building.

The man on post can reduce such thefts to a minimum by exercising ordinary precaution. Loft burglars must usually do considerable wrecking in order to gain entrance and must necessarily make some noise, and as they work while other business activities are at a standstill, the noise they make may be heard. A sound coming from the interior of a building while the rest of the lofts are quiet should be promptly investigated. It should not be taken for granted that the stock is shifting or that a cat has toppled something over.

A trick often used by loft burglars to gain entrance to a building, is to cut the padlock away with heavy clippers, substitute a lock of the same style as the old one but to which they have the keys, and boldly enter at their leisure. Try to familiarize yourself with the patterns of the locks used, as far as possible, and turn them when you first try them in such a way that you will be able to tell on your succeeding rounds if they have been tampered with during your absence.

Be suspicious of persons engaging you in conversation and of men removing merchandise from a building during hours when business houses are generally closed or immediately upon opening up in the morning.

Safe Burglars.

Safe burglars, as a rule, know the particular make of each safe on which they intend to operate. Like loft burglars, they plan far in advance and come prepared to break through any part of a building in order to get to the safe.

They have been known, when working in an exposed position, to make a pasteboard safe, paint it to imitate the original, shove the genuine safe into an inner room and leave the substitute in its place. Others do not resort to this subterfuge but simply bodily shove the safe into a position where they cannot be observed from the street and begin operations. They try not to use explosives. The easiest way, the combination, is tried first. If this fails, the weakest part, the bottom or back is tried. The ordinary safe is turned upside down and the bottom or back is cut out with a tool they call a "can-opener." If the bottom or back resists, they drill a hole near the combination and try to disturb the tumblers enough to turn the lock. As a last resort, a hole is drilled and charged with explosive. To deaden the report, the safe is wrapped with material found on the premises or blankets which they have brought with them. Like burglars who break windows or side lights, they wait until the rumble of a passing car or vehicle will drown the sound of the explosion.

A look-out is generally stationed on the outside to signal a warning, if there is any danger of being detected. The burglars are usually sharp enough to plan a means of escape or "get-away" other than the point at which they entered, and are prepared for an attack from any direction.

As in the case of house burglars, if you find safe burglars at work, try to have the building surrounded in order to cut off their escape, for, if you run in through the front door, they will escape through the rear, or vice-versa. When a building is surrounded in a case of this kind, stop any person who attempts to leave an adjoining building; he may be one of the men you are after.

In examining a safe which has been handled by thieves, do not destroy possible finger prints or impressions that may be on it.

Store Burglars.

Store burglars generally gain entrance through a rear or side window, hall door, or trap door from the cellar. They travel in gangs of two or three, one always on guard, and steal from the till, cash register or small safes. They, too, have their work planned in advance, and know just what to do when they enter.

The loot is seldom removed through the front of the building; it is carried through the rear yards or over the roofs to an adjoining building and thence to the street.

If the booty is too bulky to transport on their persons, a push cart is hired or stolen for the purpose, or a milk or bakers' wagon is pressed into service, sometimes with the consent of the driver, and the goods moved early in the morning, during the hours when milkmen and bakers are making their deliveries, so as not to excite suspicion.

Keep a close watch on stores at night, as well as the hallways of buildings adjoining and in the rear. It is a simple matter, for instance, for a thief to enter a hallway of a tenement on First Street, scale the rear fence into the yard of a store facing on Second Street and after prying open a rear door or window return with his haul the way he came, without appearing on the street in front of the store.

Try to know by sight the drivers of vehicles making early morning deliveries, and, if you see a strange or suspicious wagon passing over your post, make immediate investigation.

Store Window Burglars.

Burglars who break store windows and side lights work in pairs and are very tricky. Their outfit in most instances consists of a long piece of heavy wire and a heavy piece of cloth, such as part of a bed comforter, which they carry wrapped about their bodies.

A store is selected which displays articles of some value in its windows. The habits of the man on post are learned, and at an opportune moment during his absence they will throw a padded brick or iron through the window or side-light, having first placed the comforter on the stoop or walk to catch the broken glass and deaden the sound. Or, they may use a glass cutter to remove a section of the window. This step accomplished, they dart into a nearby hallway and wait to see if the breaking of the glass has attracted attention. If they find it has not, operations are resumed and the contents of the show window extracted by means of a stiff wire, the tip of which has been bent into a hook.

The store selected is often covered by the crooks for hours, sometimes from an adjoining precinct or post, awaiting a suitable opportunity, absence of passers-by and the passing of an elevated train or surface car or some heavy vehicle which will make enough noise to deaden the crash.

Burglars of this class usually loiter near the store they have chosen, which is, of course, one displaying stock in its windows. If you observe someone on your post or on the adjoining post or precinct whose actions appear suspicious, notify the station-house so that a detective may be assigned or the men on post in the vicinity notified. If possible, look the suspect over; you may find burglars' tools in his possession.

If you hear the crash of glass on your post or discover a broken window, make an immediate search of the hallways in the vicinity.

Vacant House Burglars.

Such thieves use the most convenient means of gaining entry; through the cellar, through the roof scuttle, or by mounting the fire-escape until an unfastened window ,is reached. Their main object is to steal the plumbing fixtures and lead pipe, although they will take anything readily portable and easily disposed of to second-hand or junk dealers. They may hide the loot near the building, in the yard or on the roof, and remove it at night; or if they take it away during the day time may carry it in a bag or openly under pretense of being mechanics.

If you discover property being removed under these circumstances, and can safely do so, see what disposition is made of the goods, and in this way get evidence against the receiver.

"Wood Merchants."

Many of the unemployed gather empty barrels and boxes from the business sections of the city, which they break up and peddle in the tenements as kindling. With the big bundle of wood on their shoulders and their shabby clothing, they excite sympathy rather than suspicion. They will bear watching, however, for the majority of them are petty thieves and steal when the opportunity presents itself, both in the tenements and in the business houses.

"Line-up" Men.

Many of the "line-up" men, who go from yard to yard in the tenement districts, soliciting orders for putting up clothes lines on poles, are thieves, and will steal anything of value within reach. In this guise, they climb the fire-escapes, soliciting orders on each floor and knocking at the windows to attract the attention of those within. If they are offered an order, they make their price so high that their bid is refused, and continue up or down the fire-escape until they reach a window where no response is made to their knocking. Assuming that no one is at home, they enter, and work in a manner similar to that of the regular flat thief.

If your attention is called to one of these men, watch his actions, investigate and look him over carefully for the proceeds of a possible larceny.

Use of Street Cars as an Aid.

The sharpest and most successful burglars of late have been foreigners, some of whom cannot speak English. Their favorite method is to select a residence along some street car route, enter it during the daytime, if possible, and remain secreted in areaways, back yards or on roofs until night, then force an entrance through a window, door or roof scuttle when the occupants have retired. After securing the plunder they open the front door and wait inside until a street car passes, then they run out and board the moving car, watching, meanwhile, to see if they are being pursued. Sometimes they ride almost to the city line before getting off the car. They are afraid that if they pass a brightly lighted street corner they will be observed by the patrolman on patrol or on fixed post, and for this reason use the street cars. Once on the car, they feel they are safe unless an observant policeman is aboard.

If you observe someone hurriedly board a street car at night under these suspicious circumstances, make a prompt investigation.

Burglars' Tools.

A person who makes or mends, or causes to be made or mended, or has in his possession in the day or night-time, any engine, machine, tool, false key, picklock, bit, nippers, or implements adapted, designed or commonly used for the commission of burglary, larceny or other crime, under circumstances evincing an intent to use or employ, or allow the same to be used or employed in the commission of a crime, or knowing that the same are intended to be so used, is guilty of a misdemeanor and, if he has been previously convicted of any crime, he is guilty of a felony.

In making arrests for this offense bear in mind that the carrying of tools, in order to constitute a crime, must be under circumstances evincing an intent to commit a crime. For instance, if a stone mason, carpenter, electrician or other person is found with tools of his trade in his possession, it would be difficult to prove that he intended to commit a crime with them; but if a barber, clerk, or other like person, or someone previously convicted of a crime, were found in a section of the city in which he did not reside and apparently had no legitimate business with a brace and bit, jimmy, false key or picklock, in his possession, it would be reasonable to suppose that he intended to make use of such tools for the purpose of committing a crime, and he should be arrested.

Some burglars, particularly safe and loft men, have adopted the ruse of carrying their tools in a musical instrument case, usually a violin or 'cello case, believing that by posing as musicians they will pass the average policeman late at night without arousing suspicion.

BURGLAR'S TOOLS

1 Burglar's Bull's-eye Lantern
2 Cutter, Part of Sectional Jimmy
3 Padded Chisel
4 Electric Motor and Bit, used for boring Safes
5 Burglar's Jimmy, Small
6 " " " Medium
7 " " " Large, Sectional, with Ripper and Hook
8 Burglar's Flash-Light
9 Burglar's Rope Ladder
10 Window Catch Tumbler
11 Burglar's Can Opener
12 Stick of Dynamite " Dan "
13 Detonating Cap and Wires
14 False Keys and Pick Locks

If the search of a person found under suspicious circumstances does not reveal burglars' tools concealed on his person, examine nearby doorways, areaways or places into which he could have thrown them. When tools of any description are found near the scene of a burglary, call a witness and fit the tools into the imprints they have left on the building, so that you can testify to this fact. Be careful, however, not to destroy any possible finger prints or marks on the tool or instrument.

ROBBERY.

Robbery is the unlawful taking of personal property from the person or in the presence of another, against his will, by the use of force, violence or threat of immediate or future injury to his person or property, to the person or property of a relative or of anyone in his company at the time. To constitute robbery, the force or threat must be employed either to obtain or retain possession of the property or to prevent or overcome resistance to the theft. If it is employed merely as a means of effecting an escape, it does not constitute robbery.

Robbery differs from larceny in that while in the case of larceny it is more or less a matter of snatch and sneak, in robbery the theft is boldly committed in the presence of someone whose protests are silenced through fear.

If a thief commands someone to throw up his hands or to become quiet and then removes any property from his person or from the person of anyone else in his presence, robbery has been committed, even though the robber has neither displayed a weapon nor touched anyone.

If a person reports to you that he has been held up and robbed, obtain an accurate distinctive description of the robber from the complainant and try to make an arrest. If possible, ascertain the route taken by the thief and

The following description, such as would be furnished by a careless or non-observant patrolman, is not distinctive and would be of little use to the Department.

"About 30 years of age; 5 feet 8 inches in height; 145 pounds in weight; smooth face; dressed in light striped suit, white turned-down collar, black and white striped tie, black laced shoes."

The following description, furnished by a careful and observant patrolman, without being technical, singles the subject out and would be of value to the Department. Study carefully the instructions under "Identification," page 71.

"About 30 years of age; 5 feet 8 inches in height; 145 pounds in weight; sallow complexion; smooth face; high receding forehead; black hair thin on top and sides; long straight nose, slightly elevated at the base; arched eyebrows; hem of ear very thin and slightly notched near top; lobe round and separated from cheek; receding chin; high cheek bones, dark mole under right cheek bone; horizontal scar on right jaw bone; walks with a swagger. Dressed in a light colored suit, black box stripes; white turned-down stiff collar; black and white striped tie; black bull nose laced shoes; wears a signet ring on little finger of right hand."

notify the station-house by telephone. Request the complainant to go to the station-house to make a more complete report of the crime. (See illustrations on pages 148 and 149.)

Pay particular attention to the secluded portions of your post and to dark doorways, etc., where a hold-up would be most likely to occur. It is well to watch such persons as paymasters, bank messengers, cashiers, and persons entering and leaving banking institutions on your post. Be wary of men loitering in the vicinity of banks, trust companies, etc., who apparently have no legitimate business in the vicinity. They may be awaiting an opportunity to follow someone with considerable money in his possession and commit a robbery.

RECEIVERS OF STOLEN GOODS.

A person who knowingly receives any stolen property, or who being a junk or second-hand dealer receives any wire, cable, copper, lead, solder, iron or brass used by or belonging to a railroad, telephone, telegraph, gas or electric light company, without ascertaining by diligent inquiry that the person selling or delivering the same has a legal right to do so, is guilty of a felony.

Except in unusual cases, the receiver knows whether or not the property delivered to him has been stolen.

If there were no receivers of stolen goods there would be but little stealing; for a thief will not steal unless he knows that he can make some profitable disposition of his haul.

It is comparatively easy to dispose of jewelry, but a thief must know positively where he can immediately dispose of bulky property that he cannot readily conceal. Usually such stuff is immediately sold to unscrupulous dealers who carry goods of the same kind in stock; for instance, a quantity of stolen cloth may be sold to a dishonest dry goods merchant. In some cases, however, a store or flat is rented in advance of a burglary or theft and the loot stored in it. The receivers are then visited in turn by the thieves, shown samples, and bids are requested. In this way they dispose of the goods more profitably.

A careful thief destroys, as soon as possible, all marks of identification; but if he has not done so, the receiver takes that precaution as soon as the stolen property comes into his possession.

Merchandise handled under unusual conditions should immediately suggest *receivers* to you. For instance, if you saw a large quantity of silk being taken into a small retail store, or saw the delivery being made from a hand-truck or from a wagon not ordinarily used for such deliveries, or by persons who, from their appearance and manner of handling the merchandise, did not seem to be engaged in the business; or if you observed boxes of shoes being taken into a barber shop, or a great quantity of food being delivered to a dwelling, it should arouse your suspicion. If you find merchandise of a peculiar kind on sale in a place or by a person not ordinarily dealing in articles of that kind, such as a bartender offering for sale a quantity of razors, or a barber trying to dispose of a stock of underwear, investigate.

Remember that persons engaged in a legitimate business are constantly devising ways and means of advertising themselves. They want everyone to know that they are engaged in a certain business, and located at a certain place, and invite inspection of their stock. They do not paint their windows to hide the contents of their store, or arrange the interior so that the stock will not be in plain sight, or deny prospective purchasers the privilege of examining their stock.

In addition to receivers of this type, stolen property is purchased as a side line by many second-hand dealers, junk shops, pawn shops, auctioneers, and stores where jewelry is sold or repaired. Dealers of this type who are licensed to purchase or loan money on second-hand articles are required, under the law, to make, at the time of receipt and disposal of such property, a record of the transaction, which record is open to the inspection of any peace officer.

Be suspicious of persons entering and leaving such places. If you find anything to confirm your suspicions and you are unable to cope with the circumstances, notify the station-house so that a detective may be assigned to investigate.

CHAPTER IX.

MANNER IN WHICH THIEVES OPERATE.

REPORT OF THEFTS AND ARREST OF SUSPECTED THIEVES.

In general, you are required to report as soon as possible any theft on your post. In seeking information, always question the individual who is in a position to give the most complete data; in a store, the proprietor; in a private dwelling or apartment, the housewife; in a tenement (if a particular apartment is not concerned) the janitor. You will generally find that the persons suffering the loss are very much excited, and that they do not answer coherently the questions you ask. Keep composed. Remember your object, and try to find out all you can of the circumstances surrounding the theft, so that the members of the Department who take up the case from your report will be able to proceed intelligently. If you do not make a memorandum of all the material facts, it will be necessary to send another officer to find them out before the Department can proceed efficiently.

A great deal of judgment must be used at the scene of the crime. It may be found that if you arrest the thief on suspicion immediately, and before sufficient evidence has been obtained to justify it, he will escape conviction; for, when a crook knows he is suspected, he will not do anything to corroborate those suspicions. In such a circumstance, you must immediately telephone the facts to the station-house so that a detective can be assigned to the case. Being in plain clothes, and his identity not known, he can secure evidence which you, with your office known, might not be able to obtain.

If you are suspicious of anyone, do not show it. Persons who are justly the object of suspicion generally make the mistake of trying to explain to you the reason they should not be suspected. Agree with persons of this kind; set them at ease by assuring them of your belief in their innocence.

Pickpockets.

Pickpockets, as a rule, try to find out the value of the property they contemplate stealing, as well as the particular part of the clothing in which it is located. When they act they must do so quickly, and they do not want to put their hands into empty pockets or steal property which is not worth the risk. They loiter in banks, railroad offices and stations, ferries, and other public places, knowing that patrons will take out their pocketbooks and expose the contents. Having located an individual with a tempting "roll" they watch him closely until they have seen the money or wallet replaced. They may then follow that person for hours, waiting for an opportunity to jostle him, until they get him in a crowd, or entering or leaving a car. They pay particular attention to travelers entering and leaving the city, reasoning that such persons intend to spend money and are very likely to have it with them. They work in and around large crowds gathered to watch a bulletin board, window display, street fight, or accident. The attention of such spectators is generally diverted from the property on their persons, and they do not notice or resent the shoving or jostling of the "stalls."

Pickpockets generally work in gangs of two, three, or four, and separate when walking in the street, entering crowds and boarding street cars. They have a code of signals by which they warn and advise one another. They are constantly on the alert for detectives, and if one is seen the signal is immediately given.

In a crowd the thieves used as "stalls" generally get behind or in front of the victim and squeeze him so that he will not feel the hand of the thief in his pocket. The thief who extracts the property from the pocket of the victim quickly passes it to one of his confederates so that if he is caught the property will not be found on his person. If the confederate feels that he too is likely to be searched, he in turn will quickly drop it.

If you see persons whom you suspect of being pickpockets in a crowd on the street or getting on or off cars, walk up as though you were going to accuse or arrest them and you will find that they will leave the vicinity.

When arresting a pickpocket, if possible have the complainant identify the property at the scene and in the presence of the person accused, secure the complainant's name and address, have him accompany you to the Magistrate's Court and have his testimony taken. Thieves of this type take every advantage of the law. They will seek as many adjournments of their case as possible for the purpose of tiring the complainant; they will find out the complainant's social or business connections and then try to "reach" him by returning a greater sum than he has lost. As a result, in many cases the complainant fails to appear to press the charge; or if he does appear, suffers from lapses of memory when testifying. In drawing complaints against criminals of this type, request permission of the court to sign the complaint, using the victim merely as a witness. If you do this and he does not appear, the court will issue a subpoena for his attendance.

Most pickpockets, when accused, immediately try to establish an alibi. They show all kinds of documentary proof, cards, letters, etc., that they are employed in some legitimate business. Their companions come forward and try to convince you that the suspects are men of good character. They bluff desperately and try to get the sympathy of bystanders. If this does not work, they become indignant, take your number, tell you of their business and social standing, warn you of the mistake and danger of your action, and threaten you with criminal and civil prosecution. Remain firm, however, and do not let them go.

THIEVES WHO ROB IMMIGRANTS.

Many thieves who are familiar with foreign languages make a practice of robbing immigrants in and around New York City. They keep posted on the schedule of trains, steamships and boats, note the time when, and places where immigrants will land, and dress in a manner intended to deceive the alien and gain his confidence. Having selected the victim they talk with him of his hopes and ambitions, and offer their advice and assistance. They accompany him from place to place until they get an opportunity to steal his property. Sometimes these operators work on the immigrant what is known as the "switch trick." They show him what appears to be a large roll of money and suggest that he place it with his own and carry the money for all. They stick closely to the victim and when he wishes to enter a store or a lavatory, warn him of the danger of taking their valuables into such a place. Being entirely unsuspicious, he turns the package over to them and, of course, when he emerges, his newly-made friends have disappeared.

This game is practiced, not only on immigrants who have just landed, but on aliens who have been in the country for a few years and who arrive in New York for the purpose of embarking for their native land. Such visitors usually have a few days to wait for the sailing of their steamer, and in the meantime live at some immigrants' boarding house and spend their time in seeing the sights of the city.

Do everything possible to assist, advise and protect immigrants and strangers who are likely to become the victims of confidence men while in the city. If you find immigrants in the company of persons whom you suspect, stop them and find out how long they have known the suspects and where they met. If you cannot make yourself understood, take them to an interpreter.

Truck and Wagon Thieves.

Thieves of this class sometimes work in collusion with the drivers, who may supply such information as the day on which they will be carting a valuable load of merchandise of the kind the crooks particularly desire and the route they will take. At some predetermined spot, the truck is left unattended and the thieves given an opportunity to jump on the truck and drive off. Or, a dishonest truckman may disclose the route to be taken by another driver with a particularly desirable load; and from his knowledge of the driver's habits he is in a position to impart suggestions as to the most opportune time and place to steal the truck.

Truck thieves sometimes have one of their gang scouting around the wholesale sections of the city, watching the loading of trucks. When he finds a dray being loaded with goods of the kind they are after, he copies the name and address of the consignee. With this information in their possession the gang know the route over which the truck is likely to be driven and follow it until a good opportunity presents itself to steal the outfit.

Sometimes the stolen truck is driven directly to the "fence" or the place where they store the goods before disposing of them to the receiver, but usually the merchandise is transferred to a wagon of their own in a location where such a transfer will not be considered unusual. They realize that the police are promptly notified and given a description of the team, truck and property, so as soon as they possibly can they abandon the truck, usually driving it blocks in a direction opposite to that from which the stolen goods have been carried.

Another scheme used by truck thieves is to back a covered wagon, generally containing two men in the rear, directly behind a loaded vehicle. When in position, the men in the rear reach out and steal packages or cases from the loaded vehicle, using knives to cut ropes, or heavy clippers to cut wire grating, if necessary. (See illustration on page 158.)

A Package Thief at Work.

Considerable property is stolen by thieves who, under pretense of stealing a ride, jump on the tail of a loaded truck and drop packages from it to the street, the packages being picked up by confederates. Watch men and boys who are riding on the backs of trucks, even though it is apparently with the knowledge of the driver.

Light packages are sometimes removed from wagons by thieves standing in the street, carried into adjacent tenements and sold to the tenants.

THEFTS FROM DELIVERY BOYS.

The thief, as a rule, observes a boy carrying a package in the street or in a car and makes a note of the name and address of the person to whom the delivery is to be made. If the address is an apartment house or a hotel, he will manage to meet the boy as he is about to enter and represent himself as the person who ordered the goods. To throw the boy off his guard, he generally rebukes him for being late; then, if the package has not been sent C. O. D., he takes it, signs the receipt, and gives the boy a tip. Or, be may request a messenger to go on some errand for him and offer to mind the package until he returns, usually sending the boy in a direction opposite to that in which he intends to flee. A woman is often used as a confederate.

Another scheme is to telephone an order to a busy store in the name of one of their charge customers, adding that a boy will be sent for the goods. If the storekeeper is not suspicious and delivers the stuff, the thief, after making sure that the boy has not been followed by a representative of the store, meets him and takes possession of the spoils.

You should, therefore, be suspicious of anyone talking to an errand boy in the street or in a hallway. If there is not sufficient grounds for you to take action, question the boy as soon as possible as to the business he had with the other person.

Dishonest Servants

There are women who obtain employment as servants for the sole purpose of stealing all they can get away with. Such a woman obtains employment, preferably where she will be the only servant, either through newspaper advertisements or employment agencies. For the time being she is a "jewel," and so ingratiates herself that the housekeeper is assured that the premises are safe in her care. However, as soon as she is left alone in the house for a sufficient length of time, the dishonest servant ransacks it, carrying away in a grip she has provided for the purpose, the most valuable articles.

The man on post should investigate if he sees a recently employed servant leaving with her baggage during the absence of her mistress.

THIEVES IN THE MAKING.

Most of the thieves are recruited from young men who spend their time in and around places known as hang-outs, such as candy stores, cigar stores, two-and-a-half-cents-a-cue pool parlors, fake social clubs, low saloons and restaurants. In such places they form the acquaintance of professional thieves whom they see living without any apparent effort, well dressed, and, after a haul, displaying evidence of prosperity. This excites the envy of some young man and he tries to gain the friendship and confidence of the thief. When he succeeds, it is not long before the thief points out to him how easy it is to profit by stealth, and how remote are the chances of detection—that it is only the careless thief who is caught—and points to himself as an example; successful because of his prudence. Confronted with the names of those who have been caught and convicted, he explains that each bungled or was betrayed by a pal and that anyone profiting by their mistakes can succeed. If he desires to make use of the young man, he first uses him as a "stall," making him carry the tools, stand on watch near the scene of the crime, carry the plunder to a fence, or jostle someone in a crowd.

Young men, engaged in work which does not afford steady employment, become acquainted with men who are similarly employed but with whom stealing is a side line.

Lack of parental supervision is responsible in many instances. Boys are permitted to remain in the streets at will and are never questioned as to where they have been or the company they have kept. As a result of this lack of restraint, they soon form bad habits, starting by stealing from pushcarts or wagons, stealing lead pipe from vacant houses, or stealing money and jewelry from drunken men in the streets. Often they feel encouraged when they bring home stolen property and are not questioned as to where they got it, and soon they develop into general thieves.

Too much and misdirected supervision is also one of the causes. Some parents interpret every mischievious act of their children as an evidence of a criminal mind and threaten continually to have them committed to some institution. Their homes are, under the circumstances, far from pleasant, and for some childish infraction, magnified in the eyes of their parents, they are sometimes sent to a reformatory, there to mingle with hardened young thieves. When they are discharged they do not look to their parents for sympathy or advice but renew the acquaintances of the boys they have met in the reformatory. Under their competent coaching, honest employment is the last thing they will seek.

Another cause is the Moving Picture Theatre. The performance changes daily, children desire to attend each performance, and resort to petit larceny for the purpose of obtaining the admission fee. They steal money from their parents, and if they cannot get money they will steal small articles of furnishing and clothing which they dispose of to second-hand dealers and junk shops. To prevent crimes of this character try to observe junk or second-hand dealers buying property from children and make summary arrests of both child and dealer, seizing the articles and money as evidence.

A young man, lazy and depraved, may form the friendship of a prostitute, who feels that she must have someone as depraved as herself to look to for protection and sympathy and with whom to share her earnings. He soon becomes a full-fledged pimp and acquires a taste for the luxuries of life. When the prostitute eventually lands in jail or in a hospital, his source of income is gone unless he can get another girl to work for him. He will not accept employment except at some position where he can steal more than his wages and if he cannot get a job of this kind, he will steal along any line which he thinks safe.

The drug habit is another of the contributing causes. Starting with a sniff to test the novelty of it, boys soon become addicted to the cocaine habit. Such drugs, besides injuring health, destroy moral scruples, and the victims are soon unable physically or mentally to compete in the strife for honest livelihood. They must have the drug to satisfy their craving, and will commit any kind of a crime in order to get money to purchase it. With their system charged with the drug, they labor under false confidence, and will undertake any crime.

Gambling contributes generously. After a boy has lost his wages, and necessity stares him in the face or he is afraid of the questions he will be asked when he returns home, he is not in the mood to let whatever moral scruples he has left stand in the way of his stealing something, if the way is open.

A girl is often tempted to steal in order to obtain and clothe herself in the finery she sees her more fortunate sisters wearing and which she finds displayed, lavishly and apparently unguardedly, in the stores or the place where she is employed. She may yield to the temptation, and if not detected at first, she acquires a feeling of confidence so that soon, instead of simply stealing when an opportunity presents itself, she finds herself seeking the opportunity.

Whenever you see a young man in the company of associates who may tend to make a criminal of him, seek an opportunity to talk with the boy, in a friendly manner, over the dangers of the course he is following. Point out to him that not only is it wrong but that crime is unprofitable and that he is sure to be detected sooner or later. Show him that his imagination is at fault. Show him some low resort, such as a "dead-house," and point out to him the panhandlers and outcasts who frequent such places and who were once considered the leaders in their particular line of crime. His defense may be that he never had a chance, due to his early training and environment. Call his attention to some person who has, possibly, suffered from a greater handicap than he and who has made a good citizen by following the lines of honesty and decency. Wherever possible, without violating the rules of the Department, make yourself a probation officer and keep a watch over him. Encourage him when he does right, sympathize with him, and advise him when he tends to do wrong.

CONFIDENCE GAMES.

Confidence men, as a type, are clever, dress well, ape the manners and tone of men of refinement, and pose as high-class sports. Their success is mainly due to the fact that they get the victim to agree or consent to enter into a dishonest transaction, and this frequently deters him from appealing to the law. It is not often that the man on post comes into direct contact with confidence men, but if he hears of their operations, he should immediately notify his commanding officer. If you observe men of this type on your post and they arouse your suspicions, note the houses they enter and the persons in their company, or any other information that might lead to their detection.

"WIRE-TAPPERS."

The victims selected for this swindle are men who possess a few thousand dollars and are willing to risk it on a "sure thing." The affair is staged with such care that the victim, even at the end, can hardly realize that he has been swindled. He is introduced, generally, to a character who poses as the Superintendent of the Western Union Telegraph Company. The meeting takes place in a fashionable hotel, or he is taken to one of the upper floors of the Western Union Building and, as if by accident, the "superintendent" meets him and his guide in the hall. Apologizing for having an urgent appointment, the "superintendent" suggests that they meet in a few minutes in a nearby cafe. He does not keep them waiting long, and they have lunch together. After the necessary preliminaries, he agrees to withhold for a few minutes the result of one horse race that afternoon and to telephone them the name of the winner in time to bet on it.

The victim is next guided to what appears to be a high-class pool room, filled with well-dressed men who seem to be bettting large sums on the various races. He is informed that one man, industriously examining the ticker tape, is "Blank, worth a couple of million dollars," and that another individual is a well-known horse owner. The entire outfit, telephones, clerks, patrons, is only an imitation of a bona-fide pool room.

After being introduced to the doorkeeper, who promises to recognize him and admit him any time he may return, the victim accompanies his guide to the place where the telephone message is to be received. At the appointed time the "superintendent" telephones the name of the horse that has just won its race, and they hasten back to the pool room, just in time to place the bet. The result of the race is soon announced, as though it had just been received by telephone or telegraph. The victim's horse wins, but the amount wagered was small. When they meet the "superintendent" and he learns the size of the bet, he calls the victim a piker, and finally prevails upon him to obtain all the money he can and make a big bet the next time.

The scene is again set. The "superintendent" telephones the victim the name of the horse to play. Instead of winning, however, it runs second. The "superintendent" upbraids the victim for misunderstanding his instructions to play the horse for second place, and often succeeds in convincing him that the money was lost through his own carelessness. In some instances victims have again returned with more money.

"The Sick Engineer."

The dupe is first taken to a large office building in the Wall Street district and introduced to a confederate posing as a broker. The "broker" expresses willingness, and even eagerness, to buy a particular mining stock that has suddenly become valuable, naming the price he will pay for as much of the stock as he can secure. The guide then leads the victim uptown to a furnished-room house, where he is introduced to the "sick engineer." The subject of the mining stock is brought up and the engineer, apparently not knowing of the rise in value, offers to sell the lot he holds for a nominal sum. Seeing an opportunity to profitably resell to the broker, the dupe unhesitatingly buys the stock. This transaction is generally timed to take place on a Friday or Saturday afternoon, after the broker has left for the day. On Monday, when the victim presents himself at the broker's office, he learns that the man he is looking for had simply hired desk room for one day and that he departed without leaving an address. Returning to the home of the "sick engineer," he is informed that that person, too, has left for parts unknown. He soon realizes that the eagerly sought stock is valueless.

Gambling Swindles.

Meeting an "easy-mark" with a few thousand dollars, confidence men will, on short notice, stage a fake prizefight, a fake wrestling-match, or a fake gambling-house. Of these, the gambling swindle is the most popular. The victim is introduced to the dealer of a gambling-house, who agrees to play into his hand and "double-cross" the house. He is taught a code of signals and is instructed to play his hand according to the dealer's signals. However, during the progress of the game, the signals become mixed and the dupe consequently loses heavily. If it is apparent that he can raise more money, the dealer shows him just how he misinterpreted the signals, and his newly-made friends induce him to try again, giving him two or three thousand dollars of their money to play with his own, to inspire his confidence. He fares no better at the second attempt, and usually loses about the same amount of his own money as the amount the others gave him to play for them.

"Dropping the Leather."

Pocketbook dropping is one of the oldest of confidence games. It has not changed in its methods, apparently, since Smollet was fleeced by the swindle in London over two hundred years ago.

In New York the game is usually worked on immigrants and seldom constitutes more than petit larceny. It is worked with two operators. Number 1, striding past, drops a pocketbook in front of the victim, who, however is not given an opportunity to pick it up, for it is instantly seized by Number 2. At the victim's protest, Number 2 agrees to divide, and leads him to a nearby doorway. When the pocketbook is opened the contents are found to consist of one or two one-dollar bills and a Confederate or counterfeit one hundred dollar bill. Number 2 points out that it would be unwise to change such a large bill in the neighborhood, and as neither has change and as he must catch a train, suggests that the victim retain the bill until the following day, when they will meet and divide equally. As security, the victim gives Number 2 whatever money he may have with him, adding his watch or other valuables.

CHAPTER X.

PUBLIC MORALS.

ILLEGAL SALE AND POSSESSION OF DRUGS.

It is a misdemeanor for any pharmacist, druggist, or other person to sell, have or offer for sale, or give away, any chloral, opium, or any of its salts, alkaloids or derivatives, or any compound or preparation of any of them, except upon the written prescription of a licensed physician, veterinarian or dentist. Such prescriptions shall not be filled more than once and shall not be filled later than ten days after the date of said prescription. The prescription shall be kept and filed, and the name and address of the purchaser inscribed upon it.

When any of the foregoing drugs are sold, the container shall be labeled or a certificate shall be given the purchaser bearing the date of sale, name and address of the doctor prescribing and of the person selling the same, as well as of the person to whom such sale is made.

Any person other than a manufacturer of such drugs or a wholesale dealer in drugs or a licensed pharmacist, druggist, physician, veterinarian or dentist, who shall have such drugs in his possession, is guilty of a misdemeanor, unless authorized by the certificate above described.

This law does not apply to the sale of domestic and proprietary medicines sold in good faith and when not containing a greater quantity of such drugs than is allowed by law, or to wholesale or retail pharmacists, chemists or druggists in selling such drugs to persons in similar professions or to scientific or public institutions.

It is a misdemeanor for any person to sell at retail or to furnish to any person other than a licensed physician, dentist or veterinarian, a hypodermic syringe or needle without the written order of a physician or veterinarian. Record of such sale, giving the name and address of purchaser shall be entered in a book kept for that purpose.

The illegal sale or giving away of cocaine or any of its derivatives is a *felony*.

The mere possession of this drug by unauthorized persons without a physician's prescription is a misdemeanor.

Cocaine, heroin and other cocaine derivatives are sold and distributed in this city by men who buy them, for the most part, from sailors of ships plying between New York City and South American ports. They are sold to cocaine fiends in small pill boxes or tiny bottles and in small paper packages generally costing about 25 cents, called "decks" or "sniffs." These retailers make their headquarters in low saloons and small retail stores, where their customers call to make purchases. They are very tricky, and to prevent detection nearly always keep the drug hidden in some secret hiding place in the wall or floor or under a table.

You can readily discover any place on your post where cocaine is being dispensed by noting the character of the persons frequenting the premises. They will be mostly nervous wrecks and degenerates. If you are suspicious that any place or building is used for this purpose, immediately notify your commanding officer and give him the reasons for your suspicions.

In arresting a person for selling cocaine, seize him quickly and search him thoroughly. Examine every part of his clothing, particularly the lining; search every part of the premises, looking between mattresses, under rugs, carpets, etc.

Opium is usually obtained in the same manner as cocaine. It has the appearance of a black paste. When not contained in small porcelain jars, it is packed in the shell of the common Chinese lichee nut, which somewhat resembles a walnut.

For smoking, it is rolled into a small pill, placed on the end of a long wire, and cooked over an alcohol lamp until it assumes a brown color. It is then stuffed into a small hole in the bowl of the pipe, and the pipe is held over the lamp until the pill has been consumed. The pipe, in shape, resembles a policeman's night-stick with a bowl inserted about three inches from the end.

Persons addicted to this habit usually frequent places or rooms known as "opium joints," where a specified amount is charged for the privilege of smoking there, the keepers supplying the pipe and opium.

In making an arrest in an "opium joint," seize the pipes used and any opium or apparatus found in the premises or on the person of anyone therein. All persons found in a place used for the purpose of smoking opium should be arrested and charged with participating in maintaining a public nuisance.

GAMBLING.

Common Gambler. A person who is the owner, agent, or superintendent of a place, or of any device, or apparatus, for gambling; or who hires, or allows to be used a room, table, establishment or apparatus for such a purpose; or who engages as dealer, game-keeper, or player in any gambling or banking game, where money or property is dependent upon the result; or who sells or offers to sell what are commonly called lottery policies, or any writing, paper, or document in the nature of a bet, wager, or insurance upon the drawing or drawn numbers of any public or private lottery; or who indorses or uses a book, or other document, for the purpose of enabling others to sell, or offer to sell, lottery policies, or other such writings, papers, or documents, is a common gambler, and punishable by imprisonment for not more than two years, or by a fine not exceeding one thousand dollars, or both.

A gambling game is any game, the result of which is decided wholly or in part by chance, which depends for its interest on the pecuniary stakes at issue.

The courts have held, however, that it is not a violation of law for persons to bet on card or other games where no person is running the game and profiting by its operation.

There are several types of gambling houses—pool rooms, poker, stuss and crap houses, and houses conducting roulette and faro games exclusively.

Racing information bureaus are usually located in office buildings, and employ several telephone and telegraph operators. They are connected by wire with the tracks at which races are running and receive from each detailed information relative to the track conditions, odds quoted, horses "scratched," jockeys changed, etc., and immediately after the race, the winner and the horses running second and third. This data is promptly transmitted by the information bureaus to the pool rooms with which they have telephonic connection.

When this information is received at the pool rooms, it is handed to the blackboard man, who lists it on a blackboard for the benefit of the patrons. The blackboard has lately been almost universally discarded and paper sheets bearing the same information substituted. This change was made for the reason that the paper can be quickly destroyed if a raid is made.

Slips, containing the information posted on the board, are distributed to those in the room. If anyone desires to place a bet on the next race, he indicates the horse or horses, amount and odds on the slip and presents it, with his money, at the cashier's window. After each race, the result is posted on the board and those who have won present their slips at the cashier's window and receive payment.

The entrance to most pool rooms is heavily guarded by several ice-box doors and by men stationed at the various entrances to keep out strangers. The doors are usually opened from the inside. When a man enters the first door he must receive the O. K. of the guard there before the second door will be opened to him. The doorman generally signals his verdict to the pool room by pressing a buzzer.

If assigned to secure evidence against a pool room, it will first be necessary for you to form the acquaintance of some person who frequents pool rooms, and have him introduce and vouch for you.

After being admitted, be particular to observe every person participating in the operation of the pool room; the doorkeeper, blackboard man, cashier, clerks, telephone operators, etc. Generally, however, the cashiers and telephone operators work behind partitions to shield themselves from the gaze of those in the pool room and only a small guarded opening is left for the passing of the bets.

Make a secret memorandum of the time you enter, the conversation you had with each person participating in the running of the pool room, his description, the amounts of money you wagered, names of the horse on which you bet, location of the track, etc. See that the races on which you bet are posted on the blackboard or paper.

Whenever possible, secure corroboration by bringing a second patrolman into the pool room and having him witness your transactions. You, in turn, should witness his transactions.

In addition to betting on the races, crap and stuss games are generally conducted in pool rooms. To strengthen your case, try to play every game in operation, and secure evidence similar to that just described.

HANDBOOK MEN.

Handbooks are usually run by men who locate at some particular street corner, cigar store or barber shop, but preferably in a saloon where there is a stock ticker giving racing results. They generally have one or two men soliciting business, who are also commissioned to accept bets for them.

All bets are paid either according to the ticker information or by what is termed "paper odds," that is, the odds quoted in the papers the following day.

In securing evidence against a handbook man, in the presence of a witness place a distinctive mark on the money to be used, and have someone witness the passing of the money and the conversation held between you and the gambler. Engage him in conversation regarding the race, the odds offered, and, if possible, obtain a receipt for the money wagered, showing the amount paid, name of the horse, name of race track and the odds offered.

Make summary arrest in such cases and immediately search the prisoner, in the presence of your witness, for the marked money and other evidence.

Stuss Games.

Stuss is a game played with a full deck of fifty-two cards. From a separate deck, cards are spread face up, or a table having a set of fifty-two cards fastened face up, arranged according to suits, is used. The player selects one or more cards and places his money or chips on his selection. When the bets have been placed, the dealer permits the first player to cut the cards and from that point deals into two piles alternately, first to the dealer's or losing pile, then to the players' or winning pile, until a card of the denomination of the one selected (regardless of suit) appears, when the pile into which it is dropped decides the bet. The percentage is in favor of the dealer.

Faro Games.

Faro is played much the same as stuss, except that in faro a dealing box of wood or metal is always used.

Poker Games.

Poker is played with a full deck of fifty-two cards. Five cards are dealt to each player, from which each decides whether or not he will "stay." If he wishes to "stay" he puts into the pot the amount agreed upon, the ante, and discards as many of the five cards as he considers valueless to his present hand. The dealer then gives each player as many new cards as he has discarded. The first player bets according to his hand and the others must cover his bet each with an equal amount if they wish to try for the pot, otherwise the first bettor, without showing his cards, takes the pot. The dealer or keeper takes a percentage of each pot as his share for maintaining the game. This percentage is dropped into a box or a slit in the table, known as the "kitty." Chips, representing value according to their color, are generally used instead of money in poker.

Crap Games.

Crap is generally played on a pool or similar table. It is played with two dice. At the start of the game, the player bets and his bet is covered by the keeper or person in charge of the game. If the first throw settles on a total of 7 or 11, the player wins; 2, 3 and 12 are known as "craps" and if made on the first throw the player loses. If any other number appears, that number must be again cast before the player wins, and if a 7 is thrown at any time after the first cast, the keeper wins. A "stick man" assists in the game by pushing back the dice with a small bamboo cane after they are cast by the player. The keeper deducts a small amount from each pot won as the house's percentage.

In the majority of crap games, the onlookers bet between themselves on the results of the game.

Policy.

In policy, the players select one number or a combination of numbers running from 1 to 78. The winning numbers, 28 of them, appear on slips for distribution at noon for the morning games and at 6 P. M. for the afternoon games. For certain combinations the odds run as high as 100 to 1.

The conducting of a policy game is a felony.

Policy is played principally in tenement houses in the Italian districts. The players are mostly women and the operators are in collusion with the janitor of the premises.

In making arrests, have the building surrounded and a policeman stationed at each exit. At a signal from the officer in charge, as many policemen as are available should enter the building and seize all paraphernalia used in the game, such as manifold sheets (fine tissue papers with numbers written on them) and all memoranda. Search the premises thoroughly. Look in desks, drawers, chimney-holes and in any place where such property might be secreted. Search every person found in the premises for evidence. Every person having a policy sheet in his possession must be arrested. Policy slips and manifold sheets have been found carried in watch cases, under coat lapels, and in narrow pockets extending from the regular pockets in clothing.

Roulette.

Roulette is played with a circular pivoted contrivance, called a "roulette wheel," containing at its circumference 34 compartments, each just large enough to receive the small ivory ball used, alternately red and black, numbered from 1 to 32 and containing two blanks, the house's percentage. A cloth containing the numbers and colors marked on the wheel lies to one side and on this the player indicates his bet. After each player has placed his bet, the roulette wheel is spun and the small ivory ball dropped into its center. The ball gradually works to the wheel's edge, where it lodges in one of the compartments, deciding the bets.

In obtaining evidence, follow the general instructions given under the heading of *pool rooms.*

Method of Conducting Gambling Houses.

Gambling houses employ men, commonly known as "outside men," whose duty it is to stand on the street in the vicinity to warn those within of the approach of detectives or policemen.

Every gambling house has a certain number of regular players who follow its management about the city wherever it moves, but it is constantly necessary to replace those who drop out with new players. New players are referred to the house by men in its employ called "runners;" hotel clerks, bartenders, etc., often act in this capacity and are called "cappers." They sometimes receive a percentage of the money won from the players they refer to the house. Each prospect, before being taken or sent to the gambling house, however, is carefully questioned and investigated.

If you are observant, you should be quick to discover a gambling house on your post. The windows are likely to be screened and the front door always closed. The "outside man," generally flashily dressed, will be seen loitering in the vicinity, night after night; a number of men will be seen to enter and leave, and, when accompanied by a runner, the runner will immediately depart. Patrons of pool rooms will be observed entering and leaving between the hours of 2 and 6 p. m.; houses holding crap, roulette, faro, stuss and poker games do their principal business between 8 p. m. and 4 a. m. If anything of this sort arouses your suspicion, make a quiet and discreet investigation and report the result as soon as possible to your commanding officer.

INDECENCY.

A person who wilfully and lewdly exposes his person, or the private parts thereof, in any public place, or in any place where others are present, or procures another so to expose himself, is guilty of a misdemeanor.

Any person who as owner, manager, director or agent, leases or permits any building, room, place, or structure to be used for, or any person who advertises, presents or aids or abets in, any obscene, indecent, immoral or impure drama, play, exhibition or entertainment, which would tend to the corruption of the morals of youth or others, is guilty of a misdemeanor.

A person who has in his possession with intent to sell, lend, give away, or show, or who sells, or offers to sell, lends, gives away, shows or advertises in any manner any obscene, lewd, filthy, indecent, disgusting book, newspaper, story, picture, drawing, photograph, figure or image, or any written or printed matter of an indecent and immoral character, or in any manner manufactures, prepares, publishes, or prints any such indecent or immoral articles, or advertises or gives information as to where or how the foregoing mentioned indecent or immoral articles can be obtained or purchased, or who has in his possession any slot-machine or mechanical contrivance with intent to show or does show any pictures of a nude female, which pictures are obscene or impure, or any other obscene, indecent or immoral picture of any kind, is guilty of a misdemeanor.

A person who shall expose, post up, exhibit, or paint, print or mark, or cause the same to be done in or on any building, billboard, wall or fence, or in or upon any public place, or anyone who knowingly permits to be displayed on any property belonging to or controlled by him, any placard, poster, bills or picture which shall tend to demoralize youth or others, or which shall be lewd, indecent or immoral, shall be guilty of a misdemeanor.

A person who sells, or offers to sell, lends or gives away, or exhibits or has in his possession with intent to sell, lend, give away or exhibit, any instrument, article, recipe, drug or medicine for the prevention of conception or for causing unlawful abortion, or represents that any such instrument, article, recipe, drug, or medicine can be so used or applied, or advertises or gives notice or information of any kind when and how or by what means such an instrument, article, recipe, drug or medicine can be obtained, or who manufactures any such article, is guilty of a misdemeanor.

Any article or instrument used or applied for the cure or prevention of disease under the direction or prescription of a physician will not be considered an indecent or immoral article.

One of the most common complaints of indecency brought to the attention of a patrolman concerns the acts of degenerates who wilfully and indecently expose their persons at the windows of their rooms, choosing a location where they will be seen by females. This offense is generally committed at the rear windows of hotels, apartment and rooming houses. Women will rarely go to court as complainants in cases of this kind.

If a complaint of this sort is made to you, report the matter in full to your commanding officer. If you see the offense committed, arrest the offender; but if you do not, and cannot induce the complainants to go to court, call the matter to the attention of the owner, manager or janitor of the premises. This will, in most cases, put a stop to the practice.

In the case of a person charged with having in his possession any obscene or immoral book, picture or article, it is necessary to prove that the defendant possessed the article with intent to sell, lend, show, or give it away.

It must be proven that a person arrested for the sale of an indecent book, paper, picture or article *knew of the obscenity.* This can best be done by holding a conversation with the defendant before his arrest regarding the contents of the book or the nature of the article, or by calling his attention to the obscenity before the sale.

If, in searching a prisoner arrested on some other charge, an indecent or immoral article of any kind is found in his possession, call the attention of the court to that fact and be guided by the instructions of the magistrate as to whether or not you will make an additional complaint against the prisoner for having the indecent and immoral article in his possession.

PROSTITUTION.

A prostitute is a female who permits her body to be used for indiscriminate sexual intercourse for hire.

A pimp is a male person who lives with or shares in the earnings of a prostitute. He is sometimes called a "cadet," "watch-boy" or "lighthouse."

There are five principal types of prostitutes: The street-walker, the inmate of a disorderly house, the "creeper," the "badger," and those who work in connection with what are known as appointment houses.

The street-walker may have an apartment or a room in a tenement or rooming house, or she may take men to hotels where they register as man and wife. She generally solicits in the vicinity of her room or her favorite hotel. Some such hotels offer a rebate to the prostitute after each visit.

The pimp is usually to be found near his prostitute; in the house or on the street while she is plying her trade. He watches for detectives and warns the prostitute by a code of signals. In case she is arrested he furnishes a bondsman, provides witnesses, represents himself as her husband if necessary, and pays her fine if she is convicted. If a room is to be rented in a house where care is exercised in the selection of tenants, he rents the room, giving fake references and representing the prostitute as his wife. Patrolmen in sections where prostitutes solicit, seeing him constantly trailing close behind his woman on the street or in court, soon learn to recognize a pimp on sight.

A prostitute may be arrested for soliciting on the street under three conditions: First, when she solicits you for the purpose of prostitution, or when you overhear her solicit a male person for the purpose of prostitution; second, when you know positively that she has been convicted of being a prostitute and when you see her stopping two or more male persons on the street within a reasonable length of time, say, within ten or fifteen minutes; third, when you observe her stopping several men on the street, if she appears to be doing so for the purpose of prostitution. In this last instance, ask her why she stopped the men, and ask some of the men what she said. If she replies that she has been seeking directions to some destination, supply this information, but if you again notice her stopping and speaking to men, place her under arrest.

Be very careful not to make a mistake in displaying your suspicions or in arresting a woman for soliciting. Give her the benefit of any doubt. Do not attempt to judge a woman by her manner of dress. Just because she has blond hair, has her face powdered, and walks jauntily, she is not necessarily a prostitute. Many innocent girls possess such an appearance without knowing the suspicion it arouses.

Inmates of disorderly houses receive employment in such places through their pimps, who make the bargain and who, in some instances, collect their earnings. These prostitutes sit on exhibition in the parlors, waiting to be selected, and receive at the close of each day's business a percentage of the receipts, this percentage depending upon their popularity.

"Creepers" are the trickiest of prostitutes. Their object is to steal from the persons they solicit. Usually they work in gangs of from two to six and have one pimp whose duties consist of renting apartments and seeing to it that any possible complainant is prevented from going to court. Their apartments are located in a respectable neighborhood and the victims are generally solicited about half a mile away. They try, as nearly as possible, to solicit married men or men who are engaged in business, who, fearing exposure, will not appear in public as complainants.

After a bargain has been made, the man is led to the flat by a roundabout route to confuse him. Entering, he finds a confederate posing as the housekeeper. He is invited to hang or place his clothes in a certain position, where they can be reached by the confederate when the victim's attention is least likely to be attracted. The confederate may creep from beneath the bed and rifle his pockets, or may slide aside a panel in the wall, in front of which the clothes have been hung, and steal his valuables. Something is always substituted; if a watch is stolen, a dummy watch-case is put back; if a roll of bills is taken, a roll of paper is returned to the same pocket; or if money is taken from a purse, the purse is stuffed and returned. This is done so that the victim, who is very likely to give himself a superficial search, just patting his pockets, will not discover that he has been robbed until he is blocks away from the house, possibly not until he undertakes to make a purchase.

After committing a theft of this kind, the furniture and pictures in the flat are changed to different positions, so that the victim, if he does manage to find his way back, will be unable to identify the place. The prostitutes, if they have reason to believe that the place is under suspicion, keep away and work from one of the other flats they have rented until the surveillance has ceased.

The "badger" uses her pimp as a confederate. She frequents large department stores, cafes and restaurants, and does not openly solicit. By dropping a handkerchief, or conducting a mild flirtation, however, she causes the victim to start a conversation. She confides to him that she is married to a traveling salesman and has quarrelled with her husband over another woman. She soon suggests that they adjourn to her apartment. Arriving there, the victim finds it furnished in a manner intended to bear the story out. A photograph hanging in a conspicuous place, he is told, is her husband, and she names him, using a middle name, such as "John Henry Jones." As soon as the man is in a compromising position, the pimp rushes in, carrying a suit case initialed "J. H. J."—to all appearances having just returned from a long journey. A glance tells the victim that he is facing the original of the photograph and he is fully convinced when the woman cries: "My husband." The alleged husband flourishes a revolver and threatens to kill both the woman and the man, but the woman pleads that his life be spared and the victim, in turn, tries to settle. In the end, he generally leaves behind everything of value he had with him, and, if he is a married man and has disclosed his identity, the pimp will blackmail him as long as he submits to it.

Prostitutes who work through appointment houses are registered in such places. Their photographs are filed in an album and their physical appearance is listed and indexed. Some of them are married and living with their husbands, and others are employed at some legitimate vocation, but all use this means of increasing their income. Appointments are usually made by telephone, the man telephoning a request to have a girl of a certain type meet him at a stated time, and the keeper telephoning the girl filling the specifications that she is wanted. If the girl has not a telephone at her home, a nearby store is requested to deliver a message requiring her to call up her "aunt" or some fictitious name known to mean the appointment house. When the girl arrives she is formally introduced by the keeper to the patron, and when she is no longer required she receives a percentage of her earnings and departs.

Prostitution in Tenement Houses.

Prostitution in tenement houses is a great menace to society, for the reason that young and innocent girls living in such houses are familiarized with the vice and are likely to be enticed by the prostitutes.

The Tenement House Law is very strict and simple in regard to prostitution. It provides that any person who uses any part of a tenement house for the purpose of prostitution, or who knowingly resides in or enters any part of a tenement house for the purpose of prostitution, is guilty of vagrancy.

Make summary arrests for violations of this law.

In a case of this kind, when the prisoner is first arraigned in court an adjournment will be had to give you an opportunity to subpoena three tenants, who will be required to testify that the house in question is a tenement house within the meaning of the law.

In making investigations you will find that the majority of janitors and agents of buildings know the character of the unlawful business being conducted on the premises. Many of them receive a weekly salary for the purpose of shielding these violators. They assume an appearance of surprise when they are informed of the character of the unlawful tenant, but will warn that tenant if they believe that the building is under surveillance. In conducting such inquiries, therefore, it is a good rule to avoid disclosing your office to the janitor.

Disorderly Houses.

In addition to preventing soliciting on your post, you should notify your commanding officer immediately on discovering that a building is being used for the purpose of prostitution.

The man on patrol has a number of ways of identifying disorderly houses on his post. If he sees a succession of men entering a private house night after night it should arouse his suspicions. The keepers of disorderly houses very often have the number of the house painted on the steps or in some other conspicuous place so that patrons will not stray into adjoining houses, and so cause the neighbors to complain sooner than they otherwise would. Disorderly houses keep a list of their regular patrons, and when, from time to time, they are forced to move, the customers are notified by mail of the new address. As the visitors near the new house they invariably stop a moment and refer to their notices to make sure of the address. Most "Massage Parlors" are disorderly houses. The inmates may be dressed in nurses' costumes and the entrance present a bona-fide appearance, yet back of this masquerade a disorderly house may be running in full swing.

The best method of securing entrance to disorderly premises is by learning the password of signal used for admittance, such as "Tom sent me," or by giving the code of knocks on the door.

To obtain a conviction against a disorderly house, it must be proven that the house was disorderly and that the owner, lessee or person in charge knew of it. If you enter to get evidence, try to identify the person in charge by observing his or her manner. If he or she directs other persons or has a conversation with you in regard to your purpose, this is sufficient to prove that that person is in charge or has control of the premises. To establish that the premises are disorderly it is only necessary to prove that women were there for the purpose of prostitution. To do this, bargain with a woman on the price, and question her as to where the act can be committed, if you have not already made arrangements with the person apparently in charge. Have this conversation in the presence of the proprietor, if possible, and pay the woman the amount she finally settles on.

Most established disorderly houses have what is known as a "get-away," a secret hiding place into which the inmates flee on the approach of the police with warrants.

If the person for whom your warrant is issued is not readily found, make a systematic search of the premises by measuring the building and comparing the dimensions of the rooms. Sound the walls to see if they contain a secret chamber. Closets, ventilators and trunks are sometimes used as hiding places.

Houses of Assignation.

To obtain a conviction against a house of assignation it must be proven that persons who are not married to each other enter there for the purpose of sexual intercourse. It must also be proven that one female entered the premises with two or more men at intervals during a period of, say, ten hours, or that one man entered the premises with two or more women at intervals during a similar period; and, in addition, it must be shown that the clerk or person in charge was in a position to observe each specific entry.

Such evidence may be established in the following manner: The first officer, as he enters, calls the attention of the clerk to the prostitute accompanying him, or witnesses any conversation the prostitute may have with the clerk. The officer, in this way, proves that the clerk would have reason to recognize the prostitute if she again appeared before him. The second officer, when he enters some time later with the same woman, causes the clerk's attention to be drawn to her. Both officers must keep the prostitute under observation as she emerges from the premises so that they will be able to corroborate each other on the fact that she is the female who entered on each occasion.

Disorderly Places.

Prostitutes and pimps often resort to low saloons and restaurants, and there, with the knowledge and consent of the owner or person in charge, commit disorderly acts, such as soliciting and using profane and indecent language.

In order to establish that the premises are disorderly, it must be proven that the disorderly acts were committed within the sight and hearing of the person in charge and that he did not take any measures to check or remedy the condition.

In obtaining evidence against premises of this character, have corroboration and visit the premises several times so as to prove that the conditions were continuous.

Subpoena persons living in the vicinity who know of or have been annoyed by the disorderly conditions and who will testify to the facts in court.

PIMPS.

A pimp cannot be convicted on the uncorroborated statement of a prostitute. It is necessary, therefore, to offer additional evidence, such as proof that the pimp accepted money on his promise to permit you to have sexual intercourse with the female, or proof that he was in a position to overhear the conversation regarding the payment of money for prostitution. If such evidence as this can be obtained and the prostitute will state that she has shared her earnings with the pimp, he should be arrested and prosecuted.

Pimps often leave cards, bearing the address of the house they represent, and sometimes a fake business advertisement in addition, at bootblack, news and cab stands, pool parlors, barber shops, saloons, and with hotel clerks, with the request that the "cappers" hand a card to each person making inquiry for a house of prostitution. A commission is usually offered.

GENERAL INSTRUCTIONS.

Whenever a person complains that he has frequented a gambling house, disorderly house or any place where persons engage in business of a character forbidden by law, refer him to the station-house or accompany him there for the purpose of having his complaint taken.

If a complainant refuses to go to the station-house, get all the facts from him, the exact location, name or description of the persons participating, whether principals or accomplices. Try, in addition, to establish the identity of the complainant by having him show you letters, memoranda, etc., so that he may be subpoenaed to court. It is well in these cases to get this information as quickly as possible, for the reason that the complainant is likely to change his mind.

Whenever property of any description is seized, mark it for identification while you are in the premises by putting your name or initials on it, and have one of the members of the Department accompanying you do likewise. Enter in your memorandum book the marks of identification used so that you will be able to make proper identification in court. All property seized must be forwarded to the Property Clerk.

ENFORCEMENT OF SABBATH LAWS.

All labor is prohibited on Sundays, except works of charity or necessity; that is, work that is needful during the day for the good order, health or comfort of the community, such as the making of immediately necessary repairs, the driving of a passenger vehicle, etc.

All manner of public selling or offering for sale of any property on Sunday is prohibited, except:

1. Articles of food may be sold, served, supplied and delivered at any time before ten o'clock in the morning.

2. Meals may be sold to be eaten on the premises where sold at any time of the day.

3. Caterers may serve meals to their patrons at any time of the day.

4. Prepared tobacco, milk, eggs, ice, soda-water, fruit, flowers, confectionery, newspapers, drugs, medicines and surgical instruments, may be sold in places other than a room where spirituous or malt liquors or wines are kept or offered for sale and may be delivered at any time of the day.

5. Delicatessen dealers may sell, supply, serve and deliver cooked and prepared foods, between the hours of four o'clock in the afternoon and half past seven o'clock in the evening, in addition to the time provided for in subdivision 1.

These exceptions are not to be construed to permit the public sale or exposing for sale or delivery of uncooked flesh foods or meats, fresh or salt at any hour or time of the day. Delicatessen dealers are not to be considered as caterers within subdivision 3.

Liquor stores must be kept closed; they may not sell or give away any liquors, cigars or soda water on Sunday.

Any other store may have its doors open, although it may not be permitted to expose or sell articles on Sunday. The fact that goods are displayed in an open store cannot be construed as exposing them for sale.

Various organizations, mainly labor unions, butchers, barbers, etc., take active part in enforcing the Sabbath laws. They invariably insist on summary arrest being made. Direct such persons to court to obtain a summons for the offender. If, however, they arrest the offender and turn him over to you, treat it as you would any other arrest and take the prisoner to the station-house.

If you observe a violation of the Sabbath law, serve a summons on the offender. The goods purchased must be brought to court as evidence.

Do not persecute; you must use intelligence and good judgment in determining what constitutes work of necessity; when in doubt, take no action.

CHAPTER XI.

LIQUOR TAX LAW.

Carefully observe every barroom on your post during the hours that the sale of liquor is prohibited. See that it is closed, that no person is in it except the licensee, his servants, or members of his family, that no screen, blind, curtain or other article covers in whole or in part any window or door thereof, that there is not near or back of any such window or door, or anywhere in such barroom, any opaque or colored glass or any article or thing of any kind that obstructs, or in any way prevents a person on the outside from having a full view of the interior of such barroom and of all parts thereof.

If you observe the law being violated in any one of these or the following particulars, make a complete entry of it in your memorandum book, noting the name and number appearing on the license, and report the facts to the desk lieutenant on your return to the station-house. You will then be directed to make and sign an affidavit, which is to be delivered to the District Attorney. Arrest is to be made only when a warrant is issued.

Some saloonkeepers employ a man to stand near their entrance, whose duty it is to intercept any child who may be sent for liquor. He takes the vessel and after having it filled at the bar, returns it. This is done so that the bartender will not be responsible for the act of the third party, who is guilty of a misdemeanor.

In all cases where liquor is sold without a license or where liquor is sold to children under 16 years of age, however, *summary arrest is to be made.* In the latter case the child must also be arrested and charged with improper guardianship.

Summary arrest is also to be made if authorized persons are prevented from making inspection during prescribed hours.

Detectives and plain clothes men who are detailed from time to time to detect the illegal sale of liquor on Sunday or during the hours when the sale of liquor is prohibited, and for that purpose enter back or interior sitting rooms of hotels, saloons, and places where liquors are sold, shall not reveal their private or official identity in any way, under pain of dismissal from the force. They shall proceed in the same manner as the special agents of the State Excise Commissioner, namely: by procuring evidence, if possible, of the violation of the Liquor Tax Law through illegal sales or otherwise, reporting it and making affidavit to the District Attorney as in the case of barroom violations.

Where liquor is sold without a license, it is always best to buy it in bulk, a bottle of beer, a bottle of whiskey, or a bottle of wine. In the presence of a witness, mark and seal it, and have the witness mark it. If a chemical analysis is required, it will be necessary for you to prove that the liquor you purchased is the liquor that was examined by the chemist, and in order to do this you must prove that there was no possibility of any person changing the contents of the bottle. Watch where the liquor is taken from. The usual defense is that the liquor was bought from a nearby licensed premises. If the waiter takes it from an ice-box or counter, note that fact. You will have to prove that the liquor was obtained on the premises.

If you are assigned to enforce the provisions of the Liquor Tax Law, after entering the premises, order from the bartender or waiter a particular brand of liquor; if beer is ordered, say: "Give me a glass of lager beer." Note the conversation and any transaction that occurs, the amount of money paid, the change, the quantity of liquor, etc. Taste the liquor you are served with so that you may swear to the fact that it is what you ordered. On your return to the station-house, fill out the proper complaint blank, sign and swear to it. The complaint blank will be forwarded (through official channels) to the District Attorney.

When two men are assigned to obtain evidence, they should at all times keep close to each other, so that they can corroborate each other in every particular, such as hearing the order given, noting the conversation, the money paid and change received, the condition of the room (particularly with reference to doors leading from the barroom), liquors exposed and persons in the room.

See to it that persons do not gather or create disorder of any kind outside of or near a barroom or place for the sale of liquor on your post.

Watch such places as cider stubes, French and Italian cafes, and places selling grape juice, to see that they do not violate any section of the Liquor Tax Law.

Extracts from the Liquor Tax Law.

Places where liquors are sold shall—

Be licensed by the State Commissioner of Excise.

Display liquor tax certificate in a suitable frame in street window or, if no window fronts street, in a conspicuous place in barroom.

Have doors leading to bar or room where liquors are sold, locked during prohibited hours, except for egress or ingress of proprietor or members of his household.

Obtain special license from the Mayor to sell liquors at night after prohibited hours.

Permit peace officers and other authorized persons to inspect premises between 9 a. m. and 6 p. m., or any other time when open for business.

They shall not—

Sell to an intoxicated person or habitual drunkard.

Sell on Sundays or between 1 a. m. and 6 a. m. on week days except with special license.

Sell to any person under 18 years of age, or permit such person to enter or remain on premises unless accompanied by parent or guardian.

Sell on Election Day within one-quarter of a mile of polls.

Sell to any person whose parent, guardian, wife, husband or child over 16 years notifies proprietor in writing not to serve.

Sell to any person confined in a prison, house of refuge, reformatory, protectory, industrial school, asylum, state hospital, or any inmate of a poor house, epileptic institution (except on the written prescription of a physician of such institution).

Sell any liquors to be consumed on the premises unless having a first class license.

Sell drugs, dry goods, groceries or provisions in rooms where liquors are sold to be consumed on premises.

Have any screen or colored glass or any other thing in the store or window which conceals or obstructs a full view of the barroom during prohibited hours.

Sell from a wagon without a license to do so.

If licensed as a hotel, sell liquors on Sundays except to guests with their meals or in their rooms (this exception does not apply to prohibited hours on any day).

Sell to an Indian.

Permit gambling or disorderly conduct on premises.

Permit a woman not a member of proprietor's family to sell liquor.

If a hotel, let rooms to a prostitute or for purposes of prostitution, or to more than one party of one or more persons between 9 p. m. and 6 a. m.

Rent rooms to persons unless they sign the register in the public office and in the presence of the manager or clerk, or knowingly to persons signing fictitious names or addresses.

There are seven different kinds of licenses to traffic in liquors, as follows:

1. To sell liquor to be drunk on premises. Hotels and saloons are also permitted to sell as per Nos. 2, 3 and 5, $1,200 a year.
2. To sell in quantities of less than 5 gallons, no part of which to be drunk on premises, $750 a year. Note —License fee for 1 and 2 varies according to the population of the borough.
3. Druggists' license, to sell liquor on doctor's prescription, such liquor not to be drunk on premises, $7.50 a year.
4. To sell liquor to passengers on a train or boat, $300 per year.
5. To sell liquor from a wagon in quantities of less than 5 and more than 3 gallons, provided such person is licensed to sell liquors as described in Nos. 1 or 2, $150 per year.
6. To sell alcohol between 7 a. m. and 7 p. m. on week days in quantities of less than 5 gallons, to be used for mechanical, medical or scientific purposes, $37.50 a year.
7. For a grower, to sell liquors produced solely from fruit, in quantities of less than 5 but not less than 2 gallons, to be sold between 7 a. m. and 7 p. m. week days, $75.00 a year.

ELECTION LAWS.

It is a crime punishable by imprisonment for a public officer to omit, refuse or neglect to perform any act required of him by the Election Law, or to refuse to permit the doing of any act authorized thereby.

All election officers are public officers.

Policemen are assigned to polling places to preserve the peace and maintain order, to see that the election officers are not interfered with in the performance of their duties, to see that properly qualified electors are protected in the exercise of the right of franchise, to prevent violations of law, to arrest persons guilty of any violation of the Election Law or of any attempted violation, and to perform any other police work that may be required of them. They must not under any circumstances write in, or even handle, the books of the election officers. They must refrain from engaging in any unnecessary conversation or discussion with citizens. They must keep order in the streets, particularly in the vicinity of the polls and should mmediately notify their commanding officer in case additional force is required. They will see that no electioneering or loitering is permitted within the polling place nor within one hundred feet thereof during the hours that the polls are open, and that the provisions of the Liquor Tax Law are strictly observed.

An attempt at illegal voting, even though abandoned by the one making the attempt, is a felony.

Any person who during an election wilfully defaces or injures a voting booth, removes or destroys any supplies therein, or before the closing of the polls defaces or destroys any list of candidates to be voted for in accordance with the Election Law, is guilty of a misdemeanor.

Warrants issued for false registration must not be executed until the person named in the warrant has voted or has had an opportunity to do so. Neither must arrests for violations of the Election Law, with or without a warrant, be made until the elector has had an opportunity to vote.

The right to vote of any person whose name is on the register is subject to challenge. A person challenged, either by some elector present or by an election officer, must take the oath or oaths prescribed before he is entitled to vote.

A messenger authorized by law to receive and carry a report or certificate of any statement relating to the result of an election who wilfully mutilates same or does any act which prevents the delivery of it as required by law; or a person who takes away from such messenger any such report or certificate, with intent to prevent its delivery, is guilty of a felony and punishable by imprisonment for not more than five years.

A Deputy Superintendent of Elections has power to arrest any person without a warrant who in his presence violates or attempts to violate any of the provisions of the Election Law relating to crimes against the elective franchise. He is also authorized to inspect and copy any books, records, etc., relating to or affecting the election or the registration of electors.

The State Superintendent or any deputy may call upon any person to assist him in the performance of his duty. He may call upon any public officer, who personally, or through his assistants, deputies or subordinates, shall render such assistance as may be required. Any person who shall fail on demand of the Superintendent of Elections, or of any Deputy, to render aid or assistance in the performance of his duty, or who wilfully hinders, interferes with or delays such Superintendent or Deputy in the performance of his duty, shall be deemed guilty of a felony. A conviction in such a case carries with it the forfeiture of office.

On election days, two policemen are assigned to each polling place and if it be necessary for either of them to leave his post, he must promptly notify the precinct in which the polling place is located in order that another officer may be assigned to take his place until he returns.

Special instructions are issued to patrolmen as to their duties on Election Day and the days of primaries, registration and special elections.

After registration, it is necessary for the Police Department to verify every name on the registry lists, and several policemen are assigned to this duty in each precinct. To do this work thoroughly it is necessary to know the qualifications a legal voter must possess, namely: he must be a citizen, twenty-one years of age; must have resided one year in the state, four months in the county and thirty days in the election district previous to Election Day; if naturalized he must have his papers ninety days before Election Day, and his name must appear on the registry list.

In this state a person does not forfeit his legal address by reason of a temporary absence.

When in doubt as to whether a person possesses the required qualifications, report all the circumstances to your commanding officer, including the names and addresses of two persons whom you have interviewed.

Most of the information required in verifying the registry can be obtained from the owner, agent or janitor of the premises from which the person registered, or from his neighbors, his employer or employees.

CHAPTER XII.

INVESTIGATIONS AND REPORTS.

It is essential that you thoroughly and intelligently investigate the cases brought to your attention, because whether or not an arrest is made at the time, a full and complete report is required. In addition, if you carefully observe conditions surrounding a crime and know how to question persons who may be witnesses, several clues will develop, and by eliminating some and linking others, the key to the situation, the motive, will be found.

The first question to present itself to the investigator should be: "Do the facts as alleged exist?" The second question should be: "Are any of the functions of the Police Department involved; the preservation of the peace, the enforcement of the law, the protection of life and property, the prevention and detection of crime, or the arrest of law-breakers?" If you can answer both questions in the affirmative, the matter is one requiring investigation, immediate police action and report.

Immediately after an accident or the commission of a crime, persons who have witnessed the incident are very talkative and will readily tell you all they know of the matter; but when the excitement has passed and they realize that they may be summoned to court as witnesses and that possibly some friend may be injured as a result of the information furnished by them, they become evasive.

It will often be found that persons who are witnesses to the commission of a crime or who know how or why a crime was committed, do not want it generally known that they have given information to the police, fearing physical harm or injury to their business, and will, if they are publicly questioned, deny all knowledge. If you question such witnesses privately and assure them that their names will not be made public, they will often become fully communicative.

In seeking information from persons who appear to be reticent, do not let them see you making notes.

It is very important that you get witnesses whose evidence will be *corroborative.* In explanation: Assume that a crime has been committed on the street in front of a certain address and that witnesses are being examined. A. states that he saw the defendant running, 25 feet from the premises; B. states that he saw the defendant running, 50 feet from the premises; C. states that he saw the defendant running, 75 feet from the premises; and D. states that he saw the defendant running, 100 feet from the premises. This is good evidence, but it has not the weight that *corroborative* evidence would have—that is, if B. would bear out A.'s statement.

Familiarize yourself with the elements that go to make up legal evidence. Without this knowledge you cannot always bring forth the material facts that are necessary to secure a conviction; or, if you do come into possession of such facts you may not realize their importance until informed by your commanding officer or the court, and it may then be too late to properly present them.

REPORTS.

To your superiors your reports serve a purpose similar to that of your testimony in court. In both cases, you undertake to convey an impression of the circumstances to persons who have not witnessed the incident, and unless you are graphic enough, so that others can clearly picture the situation, you have not accomplished your end.

Enter all the material facts in connection with occurrences on your post in your memorandum book. If a report is required, it is wanted, in writing, for two purposes: for the records of the Department, and so that other members of the Department may use it as a basis from which to work on the matter. It is therefore important that even the smallest detail be included, because if the report is incomplete, it will be necessary for the detective to consult you or to visit the scene and make a second investigation.

Enter in your memorandum book in chronological order an accurate and concise record of the police duty performed by you. In addition to having this information for the record of the Department, it should be so complete that if you were called upon to testify in court a year after an entry had been made, you could readily refresh your memory from it.

POINTS TO BE COVERED IN MAKING REPORTS.

Name and address of the person in a position to supply the most reliable information: the owner of stolen property or the person who last saw it intact; the victim of an accident or assault, or eye-witnesses. Do not use the titles "Mr.," "Miss," or "Mrs." unless it is to distinguish between a mother and a daughter having the same name.

Homicide, or Cases of Possible Homicide.

Pedigree of the victim; what he was doing just previous to being assaulted; time of the assault; location; names and addresses of persons in the victim's company; manner of assault or violence used; description of weapon used, if any; name and address of surgeon pronouncing the body dead; disposition of body; full description of property taken from the body; and disposition of such property.

Assault with a Weapon.

In addition to the pedigree of all concerned; if a revolver has been used, note maker's name, type, calibre, and serial number; if a knife, club, or other weapon has been used, note any identifying marks on it.

Burglary or Larceny.

Name and address of victim; street address of the premises; floor or part of building; manner in which the building was entered; amount, value and kind of property stolen. Try to learn from the owner something about the stolen property that will make it distinctive from property of a similar kind, such as tags, maker's name, monograms or initials.

Street Accidents (Vehicular).

Name, number and address of motorman, conductor, or driver; number of vehicle, type, and the owner's name appearing on it; direction in which traveling; exact location at time of accident.

Fires.

Exact time the fire started or was discovered; part of building in which it started; street and number; size and type of building; names of occupants; name and address of owner; cause, if known; name and address of person sending alarm; names and addresses of witnesses, and whether any suspicious circumstances were connected with the fire.

Missing Persons.

Full name and address; accurate and distinctive physical description (see Identification); clothing worn when last seen; contents of clothing; habits and peculiarities of the missing person; when last seen, where and by whom.

Unconscious Persons.

Establish identity by examining names and addresses in memorandum books or papers, or by marks on the clothing; give an accurate and distinctive physical description (see Identification).

Whenever you are called upon to get facts quickly from a person who is lapsing into unconsciousness or who is about to be removed in an ambulance, do not attempt to write the complete report as you are questioning. Jot down the answers briefly, and at the first opportunity make out a report from your notes.

SAMPLE REPORTS.

STORE DOOR FOUND OPEN.

November 13th, 1913.

Tour 4.00 P. M. to 12 Mid. Post No. 26.

At 8.15 this P. M., found front door of store at 169 Fulton St., open. Occupied by James Johnson, electrical supplies. Searched and secured premises, assisted by Patrolman Edward J. Jones, 12th Precinct. Apparently nothing disturbed.

Patrolman John Reith, Shield No. 3456.
12th Precinct.

LARCENY REPORT.

November 13th, 1913.

Tour 12 Mid. to 8 A. M. Post No. 14.

At 7.30 this A. M., a man representing himself as an agent of the Consolidated Gas Co., entered the residence of John Brown, at 1695 Green Ave., and showing a badge to the owner, said that he had been sent by the Gas Company to examine the flow of gas in the building. When he left at about 7.45 A. M., the following property was missing from a drawer in bureau in bedroom on the second floor:

One diamond ring, initials on inside "J. B. to C. B."; one hunting-case gold watch, Elgin movement, case No. 65789, works No. 64534; total value, $200.00.

Description of man, about 30 years, smooth face, 5 feet 6 inches, 140 pounds, square shoulders, light complexion, large grease spot on right shoulder of coat, black laced shoes. Reported by owner. No property recovered and no arrests.

Patrolman JOHN SHEA, Shield 4678.
35th Precinct.

FIRE REPORT.

NOVEMBER 13th, 1913.

Tour 4 P. M. to 12 Mid. Post No. 6.

At 6.15 this P. M. fire occurred on fourth floor, rear, of five story brick tenement house No. 165 West 40th Street, owned by Simon Cohen, No. 150 West 45th Street, and occupied by John Samuels, caused by explosion of kerosene lamp. Discovered by Mary Samuels, 165 West 40th Street. Alarm sent from fire box 678, N. W. corner of 40th st. and 8th Avenue, by James Duff, 456 W. 40th St. Nothing suspicious.

Patrolman JAMES KELLY, Shield No. 456.
23rd Precinct.

BODY FOUND IN RIVER.

NOVEMBER 13th, 1913.

Tour 4 P. M. to 12 Mid. Post No. 34.

At 10.15 this P. M. John Nichols, 167 Front St, Captain of Tugboat Reliance, found the dead body of an unknown man floating in the East River opposite 24th St., and towed it to dock at foot of East 22nd St.

Description of body: About 40 years, 5 feet 10 inches, 180 pounds, black hair, mustache tinged with grey, dark complexion, mole on right side of neck, small scar on point of chin, cross tatooed on chest.

Description of clothing: Black coat and pants, marked Arnheim & Co., makers, N. Y. City; white vest with black buttons; white flannel outing shirt; blue cotton underwear; black stockings; tan laced shoes, size No. 9, marked Coward, N. Y.; white turned-down collar, size 16, marked No. 6745 Sunset Brand; blue tie.

Contents of clothing: One memorandum book marked "Expense Account," date in figures; one gold watch marked with initials J. H. S. on outside of case, Waltham movement, case No. 45678, works No. 87654; one handkerchief, initials J. H. S.; one russet leather pocketbook containing card marked Julius Cohen, Architect, No. 345 B'way; six dollars in bills and 84 cents in coin. All delivered at station-house.

Body viewed by Coroner Smith, who ordered its removal to the City Morgue. Witnesses: James Hall, No. 78 Seventh Ave., a fireman on Tug Reliance; Samuel Duffy, 67 Newark St., a deckhand on Tug Reliance.

No marks of suspicious character on the body.

Patrolman JOHN SMITH, Shield No. 346.
32nd Precinct.

ATTEMPTED SUICIDE.

AUGUST 28th, 1913.

Tour 4 P. M. to 12 Mid. Post No. 35.

At 6.15 this P. M., William Lawlor, 25 years, white, single, U. S., clerk, of No. 187 West 56th St., attempted suicide in a bedroom on the 4th floor of his residence by drinking a quantity of carbolic acid. Attended by Dr. James Reilly, of Roosevelt Hospital, and removed thereto as a prisoner. Witness: Mary Brown, a servant in Lawlor's household, No. 187 West 56th Street.

Searched in the presence of Dr. James Reilly, at Roosevelt Hospital, and the following property taken from him:

One empty bottle marked "Brennan's Pharmacy, 456 Eighth Ave., No. 56784, Carbolic Acid, for External Use;" one penknife; one key ring; one handkerchief. All delivered to station-house.

Relieved at Roosevelt Hospital by Patrolman John Jones, 18th Precinct, at 7.05 this P. M.

Patrolman JOHN RYAN, Shield No. 765.
18th Precinct.

REPORT OF A BURGLARY.

AUGUST 28th, 1913.

Tour 4 P. M. to 12 Midnight. Post No. 23.

Sometime between 8 P. M. and 11.30 P. M. August 26th, 1913, some unknown person or persons entered the residence of Jane Brown, 187 West 25th Street, by forcing rear basement door, entered dining room and stole from the sideboard therein, one silver fish bowl, initials J. A. B.; one dozen teaspoons marked J. T. B.; one silver soup tureen, marked J. B.; total value $60.00.

Discovered and reported by owner. No arrests and no property recovered.

Patrolman WILLIAM SMITH, Shield No. 435.
35th Precinct.

INJURED ON STREET.

AUGUST 28th, 1913.

Tour 8 A. M. to 4 P. M. Post No. 15.

At 10.40 this A. M. Mary Jones, white, 68 years, single, Ireland, houseworker, No. 150 West 52d Street, while walking south on sidewalk in front of No. 638 Third Ave., in some unknown manner fell, striking her head against a lamp-post. Attended by Ambulance Surgeon William Meyer, Bellevue Hospital, and removed thereto suffering from contusions of back of head. Wounds serious. Street in good condition. Accident report made out. Witnesses: William Brady, No. 789 Third Ave; James Reilly, No. 56 Oak St.

Patrolman William Kelley, Shield No. 764.
18th Precinct.

ACCIDENT IN A BUILDING AND CONSEQUENT ARREST.

November 14th, 1913.

Tour 8 A. M. to 4 P. M. Post No. 25.

At 3.25 this P. M. William Fowler, 30 years, white, married, Ireland, clerk, of No. 1759 Myrtle Ave., Brooklyn, fell down elevator shaft from 4th floor to basement, through a door which had been left open, and was instantly killed, in Mills Building, No. 40 Broad Street, owned by Ogden Mills Estate, No. 40 Broad Street. Pronounced dead by Dr. John Rosch, of House of Relief. Coroner Smith viewed body and gave permit for its removal to Brown's Undertaking Establishment, No. 456 Ninth Avenue. Body searched in the presence of John Brown, No. 160 Jackson Street, and the following effects were found and removed to stationhouse: One hunting-case gold watch, Waltham movement, case No. 567894, movement No. 564782; one gold chain; one penknife; one black leather pocketbook containing two cents in cash and two old coins. Witnesses: James Boyle, No. 50 Morris Street; Mary Conlon, No. 80 Rector St.

In connection with the above, arrested one Thomas Boran, 40 years, white, single, Ireland, engineer, No. 81 Dey St., N. Y. City, charged with Homicide, he having been in charge of elevator at the time of accident.

Patrolman Thomas Moran, Shield No. 5678.
1st Precinct.

ASSAULT.

NOVEMBER 2nd, 1913.

Tour 12 Mid. to 8 A. M. Post No. 12.

At 6.15 this A. M. Thomas Murphy, 169 W. 10th St., 30 years, white, single, U. S., laborer, during an altercation in the saloon of James Brown, at No. 456 Ninth Ave., was struck several times on the head with a beer glass by Thomas Dolan, 35 years, white, married, England, laborer, of No. 164 East 17th St. Attended by Dr. Merrill, of St. Peter's Hospital, and removed thereto suffering from six incised wounds on head. Wounds serious. Assailant identified by complainant and arrested. Beer glass held as evidence. Friends notified. Witnesses: John Doe, No. 18 East 17th St.; John Roe, No. 456 Eighth Ave., who were also arrested as material witnesses.

Patrolman JAMES SMITH, Shield No. 4567.
18th Precinct.

RAILROAD ACCIDENT.

NOVEMBER 26th, 1913.

Tour 4 P. M. to 12 Midnight. Post. No. 7.

At 10.45 this P. M. John Gordon, white, 45 years, married, Ireland, plumber, of No. 190 West St., while crossing 3rd Ave., in front of No. 365, was struck and knocked down by a New York City Railroad surface car No. 654, southbound, run No. 45, in charge of Conductor James Duane, 156 Rector Street, badge No. 765, and Motorman John Kelley, No. 2 Jones St., badge No. 456. Attended by Dr. Brown, of Bellevue Hospital, and removed thereto suffering from bruises on neck; not serious. Street in good condition. Witnesses: John McCahill, 198 Mott Ave., Bronx; Daniel Ester, No. 3 West 47th St.

Patrolman WILLIAM SIDNEY, Shield 4657.
18th Precinct.

CHAPTER XIII.

CO-OPERATION WITH CITY DEPARTMENTS.

The Mayor and the Borough Presidents are responsible for the administrative work of the City of New York. For the purpose of distributing this work various departments have been established by law and specific duties assigned to each. To a certain extent, the City of New York is similar to an ordinary every-day large corporation, in that the success of the whole depends upon the success of each department; and there is hardly one department, in either case, that can be a success without the sympathy and co-operation of at least one other department.

While their duties may link together two or possibly three city departments, calling for constant teamwork, the Police Department is peculiarly situated in this respect; it must co-operate with each and every one of them by enforcing such laws and ordinances as have been passed to facilitate their work.

The City is not striving for efficiency because it has an active competitor in the field; its stockholders, the residents who foot the expense and salary bills, are looking for results. They do not care for an explanation of a failure. It is cold comfort to a taxpayer who is personally interested in a matter in which two departments have been brought into play, and which has gone wrong, to know that the failure was due to only one of the departments and that the other was quite successful. Bear this in mind and do not get into controversies with employees of other departments or try to shift the responsibility or attribute the failure to them. Your duties are clearly defined and if you fulfill them, the failure of another will never reflect upon you.

The Charter provides that many of the city departments shall make certain inspections and repairs, and it is mandatory that the public permit access necessary to accomplish such results and obey the lawful orders of the Inspectors. Very often representatives of those departments are interfered with and retarded by persons acting either through ignorance or a desire to evade compliance with the regulations. Such persons are usually liable to court action, but as litigation would delay the accomplishment of that department's purpose, it serves far better if a patrolman, without the use of force and without violating the law, can enforce compliance. For instance, a janitor might disregard the warning of an inspector of the Tenement House Department to keep a light in the hallway of a tenement; but if a patrolman were to tell the janitor that it is a violation of the law and that he is liable to be punished for the failure, it would have far more effect upon him. Drivers often refuse to move their vehicles at the request of a street sweeper who may want to sweep under them; but if a patrolman tells them to move out of the way, they do so readily.

Every department is called upon, from time to time, to handle an unusual condition: the Fire Department may have a large conflagration to fight; the Department of Street Cleaning, a heavy fall of snow to remove; the Department of Health, an epidemic of disease to control; the Bureau of Highways, a cave-in of the street to repair. At such times the responsibility resting upon the Police Department for the accomplishment of the function of the other department is as great as that upon the department itself.

While it is rarely necessary for the members of any other city department to know the duties of the Police Department in order to assist it, it is necessary that every policeman know the duties and laws governing the other departments in order to intelligently assist and co-operate with them.

DEPARTMENT OF HEALTH.

Its general duties are to enforce all laws and ordinances relative to the care, promotion and protection of health. It controls the treatment of contagious and infectious diseases, and to that end has established various rules and regulations, all of which are contained in the Sanitary Code, a violation of which is a misdemeanor.

The police co-operate with the Department of Health by reporting to it all dead animals in streets or public places, and persons and animals suffering from contagious or infectious diseases, and by taking charge of such persons or animals, or their bodies, pending proper disposition. The police also co-operate by enforcing the provisions of the Sanitary Code, the principal being the following:

Permits from the Board of Health are required for the following privileges:

To keep cows;

To keep live pigeons;

To keep chickens, geese, ducks or other fowls, or kill or offer them for sale (except on premises used for farming in unimproved sections of the city);

To keep birds, dogs, cats or other small animals for sale;

To maintain a shelter for homeless animals;

To use a cellar as a stable for horses or other animals;

To lead cattle through the streets except when landed at the foot of streets on which slaughter-houses are located. (Such streets must be barricaded.) In The Bronx, Brooklyn, Queens and Richmond, if driven through certain designated streets, permits are not required;

To keep a lodging house;

To keep a bathing pavilion;

To erect a tent or camp for the occupation of any person;

To maintain house boats;

To maintain a lying-in hospital, foundling asylum, day nursery, or to be a midwife;

To sell, keep or offer for sale, milk;

To use well-water in the Borough of Manhattan;

To conduct smoke houses;

To conduct fat rendering plants;

To conduct slaughter houses;

To manufacture mineral waters;

To manufacture prepared meats or sausages;

To conduct establishments for the breaking out of eggs;

To sell, or keep for sale, oysters;

To transport swill, offal, garbage, butchers' refuse, or other noxious substance;

To pile or deposit garbage, offal, dirt or manure in any public street or place;

To gather, accumulate, store or carry bones, refuse or offensive material;

To keep a place for tanning or dressing hides, or any business which, in its operation, generates offensive vapors or odors;

To yard horses or keep cattle, swine, sheep or goats within the built-up portions of the City;

To remove manure or stable refuse in carts or wagons;

To fill in a vacant lot with street sweepings;

To remove the contents of a privy or cess-pool.

The following acts, which might be dangerous to life and health, are prohibited:

To cause or permit any human being to use a bathroom, cellar or water-closet as a sleeping place;

To keep, sell or offer for sale or transport any food, unless protected from dust, dirt, flies and other contamination, except fruits and vegetables which must be peeled or pared before eating;

To sell or offer for sale any food which is decayed;

To expose for sale in the street or outside of a store, poultry, game or fish;

To injure or destroy any hydrant used for drinking purposes;

To supply for public use, common drinking cups, free lunch forks, and common roller towels;

To sell poison at retail without labeling the receptacle "Poison";

To sell carbolic acid stronger than in 5 per cent. solution except on a physician's prescription;

To sell cocaine, morphine or opium without a physician's prescription;

To keep an animal having a contagious disease, or to remove such animal or its body without the authority of the Health or Police Department;

To permit an unmuzzled dog to be on any public highway, public park or place in the City of New York;

To place a dead horse in the street without attaching a tag bearing the owner's name;

To throw a dead animal into any public waters;

To fill in land with garbage, dead animals or other decaying matter;

To sieve, agitate or expose ashes, coal, dry sand, hair, feathers, or other substance likely to be blown about by the wind, or to shake any mat, carpet, rug or cloth where particles of dust therefrom would pass into a street or public place;

To load manure wagons on the street or to transport manure or like substance through the streets, unless covered so as to prevent spilling and transported without unnecessary delay;

To drive a horse or other animal or vehicle on the sidewalk to the peril of any person, or otherwise obstruct the sidewalk (except in driving to and from private property);

To neglect to fence in a vacant sunken lot;

To permit stagnant water or other nuisance to accumulate in a lot;

To spit upon the sidewalk of any public street, park or place, in the public halls of tenement houses, the floors of any theatre, store, factory or public building used in common by the public, or on the stairs, platform or station of a railway;

To throw any garbage, butchers' offal, blood refuse or stinking animal or vegetable matter into a street or river;

To throw refuse from ice-cream wagons into the street;

To allow dense smoke to be discharged from any building, vessel, motor vehicle, engine, etc.;

To smoke or carry a lighted cigar, cigarette or pipe on the platform, stairs, station, or in the cars of a subway railroad.

To guard against conditions which might endanger life and health, the following acts are made compulsory:

Any person, who is the owner, tenant, occupant or person in charge of any premises, shall:

Keep sufficient water-tight receptacles to contain the ashes and garbage which may accumulate within 36 hours;

Not permit such receptacle to be filled to more than four inches of the top;

Keep ashes and garbage separately;

Keep garbage cans covered;

Remove receptacles when emptied;

Tie paper and light refuse so that it will not be blown about;

Keep the sidewalk in front of premises or vacant lots free from obstruction and nuisances of all kinds. No person shall interfere with receptacles for holding ashes, garbage or paper, unless authorized to do so.

FIRE DEPARTMENT.

Principal duties:

Prevention and extinction of fires;

Investigation of suspicious fires, and general supervision over the sale, storage, use and transportation of explosives and combustible materials.

The police co-operate with this Department in the manner described under the heading *Fires,* and by enforcing the ordinances relative to fire-escapes and fire exits, particularly in public and semi-public institutions, such as theatres, motion picture theatres, dance and other public halls, hotels, etc., and by enforcing the regulations of the Municipal Explosives Commission.

Extracts from regulations of the Municipal Explosives Commission.

"By the term *explosive*, *explosive compound or mixture*, *or explosive article*, is meant, any substance or compound or mixture or article having properties of such a character that alone or in combination or contiguity with other substances or compounds, may decompose suddenly, and generate sufficient heat or gas or pressure, or all of them, to produce rapid flaming combustion, or administer a destructive blow to surrounding objects."

Transportation of Explosives.

It is unlawful for any person to bring into the City of New York or to transport, store, sell, deliver, use or have in his possession therein, any explosive without a permit from the Fire Commissioner.

Such explosive:

Must be continuously under the care of a person holding a certificate of fitness;

When sold or delivered, must be in original and unbroken packages;

Must not be delivered within the City of New York except between sunrise and sunset;

Must not be carried in a completed tunnel or subway or in any public conveyance.

It is unlawful to transport or carry explosives except in a wagon for which a permit has been issued by the Fire Commissioner. Such wagon shall be painted red, and have painted on its back and sides the word "Explosives," and in smaller type the name of the owner and the number of the permit. Entrance to wagon shall be by means of rear door which must be kept locked. Such wagon shall have displayed on an erect pole on front end thereof a flag with the word "Danger" on it. No unnecessary stops shall be made in transit. When in transit, wagon shall be in charge of two persons holding certificates of fitness. Said persons must not be intoxicated, smoke, or be reckless or careless. When wagon is standing, at least one person must be continuously in charge. Wagon must not be driven for more than one city block along any street, avenue or highway over which there is an elevated railway, or under which there is a tunnel or subway for the transportation of freight or passengers, nor through a crowded avenue or highway. It is unlawful for any person to interfere with or molest a wagon containing explosives.

Explosives, when transported on water within the City, must be in vessels having permit from the Fire Commissioner. The explosives are not to be loaded on dock or pier, but must be transferred directly to or from the wagons.

Storage of Explosives.

It is unlawful to store or keep explosives except in a magazine for which a permit has been issued by the Fire Commissioner. Such magazine shall be continuously in charge of a person holding a certificate of fitness issued by the Fire Commissioner. It is unlawful to keep a greater quantity of explosives in a magazine than is allowed by the permit. Copy of permit shall be conspicuously displayed in glass case on outside of magazine.

Use of Explosives.

It is unlawful for any person to blast unless he has a certificate of fitness from the Fire Commissioner. Permit must be had to blast at each specific location. Blasting operations must not be carried on between 7 p. m. and 7 a. m., nor on Sundays, unless with special permit. After tamping the hole, and before firing the blast, the rock or substance to be blasted shall be covered on all exposed sides with a strong woven matting of rope or wire at least one and one-half inches in diameter; the matting shall then be covered with at least twelve timbers each 10 inches in smallest diameter by 10 feet long, held securely by chains or by iron or steel cables at least three-quarters of an inch in diameter. After the rock or substance shall be thus covered, it shall be blasted without unnecessary delay. At least three minutes before firing a blast, the blaster shall give warning thereof, by causing a competent man carrying a red flag to be stationed at a reasonable distance from the blast at each avenue of approach or point of danger.

Fireworks.

"By the term *fireworks* is meant any combustible or explosive composition, or any substance or combination of substances, or article, prepared for the purpose of producing a visible or an audible pyrotechnic effect by combustion, explosion, deflagration or detonation."

Fireworks shall not be manufactured, transported, stored or sold without a permit from the Fire Commissioner.

It is unlawful to smoke or carry a lighted cigar or cigarette where fireworks are manufactured, sold or stored.

Fireworks shall not be sold or exhibited for sale on the sidewalks, streets, parks, squares, piers or other public places, or in the windows or doors of places having a permit to sell them.

It is unlawful to carry or transport through the streets, avenues or highways, fireworks exceeding $10 wholesale value, unless they are securely packed in spark-proof boxes, or to carry or transport fireworks in a tunnel or subway under the streets, land or water of the City of New York.

It is unlawful to display any fireworks, flashlights, colored fire or open lights, upon the stage of any theatre or other place of public amusement without having a permit from the Fire Commissioner.

The Fire Commissioner may issue a permit to a person wishing to use or discharge fireworks, but no permit shall be issued to discharge fireworks in a street which is less than 80 feet wide, or within 1,000 feet of a hospital. If the fireworks exceed $10 wholesale value, the person discharging them must have a certificate of fitness as a pyrotechnist from the Fire Commissioner. Permits shall be issued in duplicate, one of which shall be filed with the commanding officer of the police precinct wherein the display is to be given, and shall be evidence of the right of the person named therein to give the display.

No permit shall be required to discharge fireworks of less than $2 wholesale value on the 4th day of July.

Miscellaneous Provisions.

It is unlawful for any person to store, sell or offer for sale any ammunition except with a permit from the Fire Commissioner. Holders of permits may store a limited number of blank shells or cartridges to be used in cannons for saluting purposes; number to be stored shall be stated in permit. No permit shall be issued for the use of blank cartridges except in connection with performances in duly authorized theatres or places of public amusement. The holder of a permit for the storage and sale of ammunition must not store or exhibit in the windows or doors of the premises covered by the permit any cartridges or shells containing explosives.

Garages.

It shall be unlawful for any person to store, house or keep within the City of New York, any motor vehicle containing volatile inflammable oil except in a building, shed or enclosure for which a garage permit shall have been issued by the Fire Commissioner.

Each garage storing volatile inflammable oil shall be equipped with a storage tank, which must not be placed under the sidewalk or in front of the building line.

No barrel containing volatile inflammable oil shall be taken off the vehicle delivering such oil to a garage, but the oil shall be delivered directly to the storage tank by means of a hose connected with the barrel on the vehicle. If the oil is being delivered from the tank to a motor vehicle, it must be done by means of a portable tank, or directly through the draw-off pipe. Vehicles delivering oil of an inflammable nature to a garage must not enter.

It shall be unlawful for any person to smoke or carry a lighted cigar, cigarette, pipe or match within any room or enclosed place, or in any cellar or basement or in any part of any premises in which explosives or highly inflammable material is stored or kept for use or sale.

Street Fires.

No person shall kindle, build, maintain or use a fire in or upon a public street, avenue or highway within the City of New York without a permit from the Fire Commissioner.

No permit shall be issued to kindle, build, maintain, or use a fire,—

(a) within 15 feet of a fire hydrant,

(b) within two feet of the surface of any stone pavement,

(c) within two feet of the surface of any asphalt pavement, except for the purpose of repairing or removing or constructing the same.

A street fire maintained under a permit, must be continually under the care and direction of a competent person at all times.

Various Permits Issued by the Fire Commissioner.

The Fire Commissioner issues permits for the following:

Motor-vehicle repair shops,

Dry-cleaning and dyeing establishments,

Sponging establishments (if conducted as a separate business),

Storage, sale or use of kerosene or other illuminating oil in quantities greater than ten gallons,

Storage of calcium carbide in excess of 120 pounds,

Storage of inflammable motion picture films in quantity greater than ten reels,

Storage or keeping on hand any oil, fat, grease or soap stock exceeding five barrels.

Pyrotechinic establishments and places where chemicals and other explosives are stored or kept for sale,

Wholesale and retail drug stores and chemical supply houses,

Premises storing or keeping on hand, inflammable or combustible mixtures, including floor polishes, stove polishes, cleaning fluids, disinfectants, insecticides and similar mixtures and compounds, in quantities exceeding ten gallons,

Premises storing or keeping on hand, paints, varnishes or lacquers, in quantities of more than twenty gallons,

Premises storing or keeping on hand matches in quantity of 60 matchman's gross or more,

Premises storing or keeping on hand combustible fibres, including cotton, flax, hemp, oakum, broom corn, cotton or woolen rags, paper, paper stock, paper clippings, sawdust and similar articles, in excess of two tons.

Violations of the Municipal Explosives Commission's regulations, or failure to have a required permit is a misdemeanor, and violators are to be arrested or served with a summons.

Extracts from the Penal Law relative to Explosives:

"A person who, by the careless, negligent, or unauthorized use or management of gunpowder or other explosive substances, injures or occasions the injury of the person or property of another," is guilty of a felony. * * * "Any person or persons who shall knowingly present, attempt to present, or cause to be presented or offered for shipment to any railroad, steamboat, steamship, express or other company engaged as common carrier of passengers or freight, dynamite, nitroglycerine, powder or other explosive dangerous to life or limb, without revealing the true nature of such explosives or substance so offered or attempted to be offered to the company or carrier to which it shall be presented, shall be guilty of a felony, * * * A person, who places in, upon, under, against, or near to any building, car, vessel or structure, gunpowder or any other explosive substance, with intent to destroy, throw down, or injure the whole or any part thereof, under such circumstances, that, if the intent were accomplished, human life or safety would be endangered thereby, although no damage is done, is guilty of a felony."

TENEMENT HOUSE DEPARTMENT.

The Tenement House Department has control of all tenements within the City of New York, that is, any house or building, or portion thereof, which is to be or is occupied as the residence of three or more families living independently of each other and doing their cooking on the premises, or by more than two families upon any floor doing their cooking on the premises but having a common right to the yards, stairways, halls, water-closets or privies, or some of them. It may cause to be vacated tenements which are infected or uninhabitable through the presence of a contagious disease or on account of defective plumbing, light, ventilation or construction.

The Police Department co-operates with this Department principally by assigning a number of policemen to enforce the provisions of the Tenement House Law, and by policemen in general reporting any violations of which they may become cognizant and taking other police action when necessary; particularly by arresting persons who, in tenement houses, commit or permit to be committed acts of prostitution, or solicit for that purpose; and by arresting or summoning persons who, in tenement houses :

Violate the provisions of the Sanitary Law;

Encumber, or permit to be encumbered, fire escapes;

Being the owner, agent, lessee, or occupant, fails to have lights burning from sunset to sunrise in the public hallways near the stairways on the first and third floors, and upon all other floors from sunset until 10 p. m.;

Interfere with a Tenement House Inspector in the performance of his duties.

DEPARTMENT OF STREET CLEANING.

Principal duties:

Sweeping and cleaning of all streets (except those under control of the Department of Docks and Ferries) in the Boroughs of Manhattan, The Bronx and Brooklyn;

Removal of rubbish, garbage, ashes, snow, and sweepings, and the disposition of same;

Removal of unharnessed vehicles, barrels, boxes, bales of merchandise, and such other movable property, from the streets.

The Police Department co-operates with this Department principally by reporting all vehicles left unharnessed in the streets and by enforcing all laws and ordinances relative to street cleaning:

By arresting or summoning persons who:

Throw or distribute handbills, circulars, or cards in the streets;

Sweep dust from sidewalks into the street except before 8 a. m. or before the first sweeping by the Department of Street Cleaning;

Leave a vehicle unharnessed in the street, unless such vehicle is disabled, in which case three hours of grace is allowed;

Obstruct the free flow of water in a gutter by placing building material therein;

Neglect to remove snow and ice from the sidewalk and gutter in front of their premises within four hours after snow ceases to fall (9 p. m. to 7 a. m. not included), unless it is frozen so hard that its removal would injure the sidewalk, in which case they must not neglect to sprinkle the walk with ashes or sawdust;

Interfere with the members of the Department of Street Cleaning while in the performance of their duties;

Violate the provisions of the Sanitary Law relative to ash and garbage receptacles. (See Department of Health);

Permit dirt or like substance to drop from carts into the street.

Littering of the streets can be prevented in the majority of cases by speaking to the persons responsible and having them correct the condition immediately. For instance, if dirt or litter is found in front of a fruit or newspaper stand, or in a basement stairway or areaway, request the person in charge to sweep the premises and place the refuse in a receptacle. Serve a summons if the man is obstinate.

Such refuse as newspapers and fruit skins is generally thoughtlessly thrown into the streets. Call the offender's attention to the fact that he is committing a misdemeanor and request him to drop the refuse into one of the receptacles provided for that purpose. If he refuses and can be identified, serve him with a summons.

DEPARTMENT OF WATER SUPPLY, GAS AND ELECTRICITY.

Principal duties:

The supervision of property and structures connected with the supply and distribution of water for public use, including fire and drinking hydrants and water meters;

Enforcement of laws and ordinances regulating the use of city water;

Issuance of permits for the laying and removal of electric wires and for use of city water to sprinkle sidewalks, lawns, etc.;

Supervision over the manufacture of gas within the city;
Supervision over public lamps (gas or electric).

The Police Department co-operates with this Department mainly by reporting all public lamps broken or not lighted at the proper time, breaks in the water-mains or fire-hydrants; by preventing persons from wasting public water; by arresting or summoning persons who, without a permit from the Commissioner of the Department of Water Supply, Gas and Electricity,

Operate a moving picture machine;
Open or use a fire hydrant (except the Fire Department);
Take up, break, or remove a public lamp;
Open the street to connect with a water main;

and by reporting to the Corporation Counsel persons who; without having the proper permit,

Use water to sprinkle sidewalks, lawns, etc.;
Take city water from any public water connection to use on boats or ships.

DEPARTMENT OF PARKS.

Principal duties:

Control of all public parks and squares;
Supervision over boulevards, driveways, parkways, etc.

Policemen are assigned to the various parks to enforce the laws and ordinances applying to them, and in addition the Police Department co-operates with the Department of Parks by arresting or summoning persons who, in any park, street, or public thoroughfare within the city limits, without a permit from the Park Commissioner,

Cut down a tree, or trim its branches;
Attach guy ropes to a tree,
Plant a tree; or
Injure or destroy a tree in any manner.

DEPARTMENT OF DOCKS AND FERRIES.

Principal duties:

Control over all docks, ferries, wharves, lands under water, and all water adjacent to the City of New York;

Assignment of piers for the use of the Fire Department, the Department of Health, and the Department of Street Cleaning; also for Public Baths, and Recreation Piers.

The police co-operate with this Department by maintaining order at public baths and recreation piers, and by arresting or summoning persons who unlawfully dump refuse or throw dead animals into tidal waters within the city limits.

DEPARTMENT OF EDUCATION.

Principal duties:

Establishment and maintenance of public school houses;

Supervision and control of public schools and high schools;

Enforcement of the Compulsory Education Law, through its truant officers.

The Police co-operate with this Department, principally as follows:

By enforcing the provisions of the Compulsory Education Law, in seeing that every child between 7 and 14 years of age who is able to attend school, does so;

By enforcing the provisions of the Child Labor Law;

By preventing boys under 12 years and girls under 16 years from selling newspapers or magazines in public streets or places;

By preventing boys between the ages of 12 and 14 years from selling newspapers or magazines without permit and badge from the Board of Education;

By preventing children under 16 years from selling newspapers after 8 p. m. and before 6 a. m.;

By arresting or summoning persons who make unnecessary noise in school streets;

By arresting or summoning persons who endanger the lives of children by reckless driving in the vicinity of schools;

By arresting or summoning persons who drive vehicles through a school fire drill or in any manner interfere or obstruct same;

By stationing policemen at school crossings for the protection of children going to and coming from school.

DEPARTMENT OF PUBLIC CHARITIES.

Principal duties:

Supervision and control of all public institutions belonging to the City of New York, devoted to the care of the sick, destitute, blind, infirm, or feeble-minded (except the institutions on Ward's Island, and those under the control of the Department of Health and Bellevue and Allied Hospitals), and institutions for the temporary care of vagrants;

Enforcement of the law relative to children born out of wedlock.

The police co-operate with this Department, mainly as follows:

By reporting to it all persons in need of charitable aid;

By directing applicants to the proper institutions for their care;

By executing warrants in bastardy cases;

By arresting persons who abandon their families in destitute circumstances;

By seeing that unclaimed dead bodies are taken to the morgue.

DEPARTMENT OF CORRECTION.

Principal duties:

Supervision and control of all institutions for the care and custody of prisoners in the City of New York—*except* the House of Refuge, the House of Detention for Witnesses, the Brooklyn Disciplinary Training School, and the Society for the Prevention of Cruelty to Children. There is no branch of the Department of Correction in Richmond; in this borough the custody of prisoners awaiting trial is in the hands of the Sheriff.

The police co-operate with this Department, as follows:

By turning over to it prisoners who have been held in the Magistrates' Courts;

By arresting persons who violate their parole after being discharged from the New York City Reformatory; and

By arresting escaped prisoners.

DEPARTMENT OF BRIDGES.

Principal duties:

Supervision of the construction, maintenance and repair of all bridges which cross navigable rivers or which have a terminus in each of two boroughs.

The police co-operate with this Department mainly by enforcing all laws and ordinances relative to bridges, and by regulating traffic on the bridges and at their terminals.

LAW DEPARTMENT.

The Corporation Counsel is the head of this Department.

Principal duties:

- Conduct of all legal proceedings in which the interests of the city are involved; and
- Giving of legal opinions to all city departments, boards or officers, in connection with city affairs.

The police co-operate with this department principally by reporting to the Corporation Counsel all violations of Corporation Ordinances in which the penalty is to be recovered by civil suit, and by investigating, procuring witnesses, reporting and recording all accidents to persons or property in which the City of New York may be involved.

BOROUGH ADMINISTRATION.

The following bureaus are under the control of the Borough President. The heads of these bureaus are appointed by him and act under his supervision:

- Bureau of Highways,
- Bureau of Sewers,
- Bureau of Buildings,
- Bureau of Encumbrances,
- Bureau of Public Buildings and Offices,
- Bureau of Public Baths and Comfort Stations.

BUREAU OF HIGHWAYS.

Principal duties:

Regulation of the grading, curbing and flagging of streets, the laying of crosswalks, the construction and repair of public roads, laying and relaying of surface railway tracks in public streets or roads, method of construction and quality and kind of material used in the above, and the issuance of permits to builders and others to open public streets or to use them for special purposes.

The police co-operate with this Bureau principally by enforcing the laws and ordinances relative to the use of public streets, by reporting sunken or unsafe street and sidewalk pavements, and by reporting to the Corporation Counsel persons who, without having a permit from the Borough President,

Open any street pavement;

Erect a bridge or roof over sidewalk (except a shed over the sidewalk when erecting a building over 65 feet high);

Place building material on the street, or violate the provisions of their permit by placing building material within two feet of a railway track, four feet of a lamp post, or ten feet of a fire hydrant, or by occupying more than one-third of the width of the roadway with it, or by failing to place lights on such material at night;

Close a public street or sidewalk, or, having a permit to do so, do not leave room for pedestrians to pass, or otherwise violate the provisions of such permit;

Build a vault or cistern under sidewalk;

Move a building through or across any street;

Place an awning of tin, light metal, or canvas, across sidewalk, except temporary canvas awnings during inclement weather;

Take up or remove sidewalk or any part thereof, paved with granite, blue stone flagging, or artificial stone, except to reset it or to repair coal chute under sidewalk; or

Change grade of sidewalk for the purpose of maintaining a carriageway;

—by reporting to the Corporation Counsel persons who:

Neglect to place fences or barriers around excavations in the streets or public places;

Fail to have necessary lights burning on such excavations at night;

Do not cover vaults with suitable cover having a rough surface; or

Obstruct street water-gates by placing building material on them;

—and by arresting or summoning persons who:

Place building material or mix mortar or like substance on a street paved with asphalt, wood or asphalt blocks unless such pavement is protected with planking; or

Obstruct a sidewalk or crosswalk unlawfully.

BUREAU OF SEWERS.

Principal duties:

Control of all matters relating to public sewers and drainage of the borough.

The police co-operate with this Bureau principally by reporting all broken manholes, culverts, sewers and basins, and by arresting or summoning persons who:

Throw garbage or dead animals into sewers; or

Permit combustible material to flow into sewers;

—by preventing persons, who have not the necessary permit from the Borough President, from

Making connection with a sewer or drain;

Placing heavy weights on wharves or bulkheads upon the sewer outlet, when such outlet is within three feet of the surface; or

Breaking or removing manhole covers;

—and by reporting such violations to the Corporation Counsel.

BUREAU OF BUILDINGS.

Principal duties:

Supervision of the construction, alteration and repair of all buildings and enforcement of the building laws.

The police co-operate with this Department by reporting unsafe buildings; by causing unsafe buildings to be vacated and safeguarded, if necessary; by reporting to the Corporation Counsel persons who, without a permit from the Superintendent of Buildings,

Build, alter, or demolish a building;

Remove more than one story at a time when demolishing a building; or

Erect any temporary structure, such as a sky sign, billboard, shanty, etc.;

—and by reporting to the Corporation Counsel persons who

Fail to take proper precautions to prevent accidents while demolishing or erecting buildings; or

Fail to protect pedestrians by putting a shed over the sidewalk when erecting a building more than 65 feet high.

BUREAU OF ENCUMBRANCES.

Principal duties:

The removal of all encumbrances from the streets and public places except such encumbrances as the Department of Street Cleaning must remove.

The police co-operate with this Depertment by reporting all encumbrances in streets or public places and by taking necessary police action against the persons responsible.

LICENSES.

Licenses are required from various city and state departments to conduct certain businesses specified below. The Police Department co-operates first, by seeing that no business requiring a license is conducted without one; and second, by seeing that persons conducting a business under a license comply with the provisions of the law regulating that particular business.

Businesses requiring Licenses from the Department of Licenses.

Common Shows. These are deemed to include: a carousel, gravity steeplechase, scenic railway, switchback, puppet show, Ferris wheel, chute, striking machine, merry-go-round, ball game, and all other shows of like character, but not to include games of baseball or to authorize gambling or any games of chance.

Dirt Carts. They shall have the words "Dirt Cart" or "D. C." and license number on vehicle; have tight box and be securely covered when loaded to prevent contents from spilling.

Express (and Expressmen). Express wagons shall bear the word "Express" or "Exp." and license number; shall not be driven except by licensed express drivers, nor charge more than the legal rate.

Hand Organs. In the Borough of Brooklyn, hand-organ players must display their license conspicuously. They shall not play on Sunday or between 9 p. m. and 9 a. m. on other days; shall not play within 500 feet of a school or church during school hours or hours of public worship, nor within 250 feet of buildings where occupants object. In the Borough of Manhattan shall not play after 7 p. m., or before 9 a. m.

Employment Agencies shall: obtain a license from the Commissioner of Licenses; keep a register containing the name and address of each applicant, nature of employment sought and fee received; and return all fees to applicant on demand after three days if employment has not been secured for them.

They shall not: charge more than 10% of the first month's wages for securing employment; maintain an employment agency where boarders or lodgers are kept; send applicants for employment to disorderly houses or gambling houses.

Hoist (Exterior). Persons generally engaged in the business of hoisting must have a general hoist license. If hoisting in front of certain premises only, a special hoisting license or permit is required.

When hoisting or lowering over a sidewalk or public place, two conspicuous warning signs are to be displayed with the word "Danger" appearing thereon.

Junk Carts. Junk carts shall have the word "Junk Cart" and license number displayed on vehicle.

Junk Dealers and Second-Hand Dealers shall both keep a book and enter therein at the time of purchase, a description of every article bought, the name and address of seller, and the date and time of purchase. They shall give information to the Police Commissioner in writing of any article in their possession which is advertised as lost or stolen, and are compelled to exhibit to the Mayor, Commissioner of Licenses, any police officer or magistrate, or any one authorized in writing by any of them, any article alleged to have been lost or stolen, and their books and records.

They shall not: bny anything from a child under 16 years of age, or from an apprentice or servant; buy anything on Sundays, or between sunset and 7 a. m. on any other day; nor shall they buy or receive any wire, cable, copper, lead, solder, iron or brass used by or belonging to a railroad, telephone, telegraph, gas or electric light company, without ascertaining by diligent inquiry that the person selling the same has a legal right to do so. A violation of this last clause is a felony.

Second-hand dealers shall not be licensed as junk dealers or pawnbrokers; nor shall they sell any merchandise purchased, except kitchen utensils, stoves and wooden furniture, until one month from time of purchase; nor shall they receive any article by way of pledge or pawn.

Moving Picture Shows. No child under 16 years of age shall be permitted to enter or remain therein unless accompanied by parent or guardian. No pictures shall be shown on Sunday unless they are of an educational or instructive character.

Pawnbrokers shall enter in a book the time of pledging, a description of the article pawned, amount loaned, name and address of the person pawning; they shall give person pawning, a ticket containing substance of entry; if the rightful owner loses a ticket, they shall give him a second one; shall exhibit stolen property to the true owner on demand, and permit the Mayor, judges of criminal courts, the Police Commissioner, Inspector or Captain of Police, or any person authorized by them, to examine their books and property.

They shall not take anything in pledge or pawn from a child under 16 years; sell articles pawned until the expiration of a year, and then at public auction; shall not do business on Sunday or before 7 a. m., or after 6 p. m., except Saturdays, when they may do business until midnight.

Peddlers. Including persons hawking, vending and selling wares, except periodicals and newspapers. In the Borough of Manhattan, peddlers shall show their license to any person on demand; wear their license badge conspicuously displayed while peddling; and if using a push-cart or vehicle, use east and north side of streets and avenues until noon, and south and west sides after noon, and also have the words "Licensed Peddler" and number of license on vehicle.

They shall not: blow or use any horn or make any other unnecessary noise; if peddling from a vehicle, stand within 25 feet of crosswalks; use any part of sidewalk or crosswalk to transact business; interfere with the Department of Street Cleaning; if peddling from horse and wagon, employ more than two assistants; cry or sell their wares on Sunday, or before 8 a. m. or after 9 p. m. on other days (except Saturday, when they may sell until 11.30 p. m.); or cry their wares within 250 feet of a hospital, church, court, or school, between 8 a. m. and 4 p. m.; or stand in front of any building when the owner or lessee of ground floor objects; nor in streets or highways where peddling is prohibited.

Pool Parlors. Premises to be conducted in an orderly manner. Children under 16 years not to be permitted to play therein, or to enter unless accompanied by parent or guardian.

Public Carts shall have the words "Public Cart" and license number on vehicle; shall be entitled to legal compensation after transportation and before delivery, and if not paid, have the right to retain the whole or part of the load and place same in a storage warehouse; disputes relative to legal compensation shall be settled by officer in charge of police station nearest to where dispute occurred.

Public Bowling Alleys. Premises to be conducted in an orderly manner. Children under 16 years not to be permitted to bowl therein, or to enter unless accompanied by parent or guardian.

Public Dance Halls. A public dance hall is any place where dancing is permitted and to which admission may be had by the payment of a fee or the possession of a check for the caring of clothing, for which a charge has been made; or any place where dancing is permitted and which is licensed to sell liquor, whether or not an admission fee is charged. This law does not apply to hotels having 50 or more bedrooms, or to dance halls where the people who pay to enter do not participate in the dancing. Inspectors of Dance Halls, appointed by the Mayor, shall have access to premises at all reasonable times.

The license must be displayed in a conspicuous place.

Public dance halls shall not: permit children under 16 years of age to enter or remain therein unless accompanied by parent or guardian; sell or give away beer or liquors if dancing is taught in the premises, or if it is announced that dancing is taught; or permit disorderly or immoral acts to be committed on premises.

Public Porters shall wear the prescribed badge. They shall not give such badge to any other person to wear, nor charge more than the legal rate.

Stands within Stoop Lines or under Elevated Stations shall display the proper license on the stand; the former shall be strictly within stoop line and not obstruct sidewalk; and sell only newspapers, periodicals, fruit and sodawater, or be for the shining of shoes.

Stands within stoop lines shall not be more than ten feet long and four feet wide; or transfer the license to another person except with permission of the Department of Licenses. Boot-black stands shall not have more than three chairs, 3 x 4 feet in size, nor shall any stand under elevated stairs be wider than the width of stairs.

Note: No license is required for stands within stoop lines for the sale of newspapers or periodicals, when such stands are conducted by a newsdealer who is the owner or occupant of the premises in front of which they are located.

Theatres, Concert Halls and Circuses shall be conducted in an orderly manner; conform to regulations of the Fire Department, and the Bureau of Buildings; and give no indecent or immoral performance.

They shall not permit any child under 16 years of age to enter or remain therein unless accompanied by parent or guardian.

Concert Halls shall close at 12 o'clock Midnight, and not reopen until 6 a. m.; shall not allow females to serve refreshments or allow performers to mingle with audience.

They shall not: permit aisles or passageways to be obstructed; permit any child under 16 years to enter or remain therein unless accompanied by parent or guardian; give any performance on Sunday except moving pictures of an educational or instructive character or vocal and instrumental concerts, lectures, recitation and addresses; sell any wine, beer or spirituous liquors except where concerts consisting of vocal and instrumental music are given, and then only with permission of the Police Commissioner; employ women to furnish refreshments, or mingle with audience; give any immoral play or exhibition, or give any play or exhibition representing the Divine Person by a living character.

Licenses issued by Departments other than the Department of Licenses.

Auctioneers shall: have a license from the City Clerk; sell between sunrise and sunset only, and not on Sundays; have special permission from the Department of Licenses to sell after sunset; sell after sunset only books, prints, statuary, works of art, and goods which are in original manufacturers' packages; and previously advertise sales in one or more daily papers.

They shall not: conduct any mock auctions; permit any other person to sell for them; sell goods to persons who are standing on the sidewalk while bidding for or examining goods; or attract the attention of persons to the auction by employing bellmen, criers or musical instruments.

Engineers shall obtain a license from the Police Commissioner to be in charge of any stationary engine carrying more than 10 pounds of steam.

They shall not cause boilers to burst by over-pressure, ignorance or carelessness, nor carry more steam in any boiler than is allowed by boiler certificate.

Immigrants' Boarding Houses shall be licensed by the State Labor Department and give bond; they shall also display license in a conspicuous place.

Liquor Dealers. (See Liquor Tax Law.)

Motor Vehicles and Operators. Motor vehicles shall: be licensed by the Secretary of State; display prescribed number plates, one in front and one in rear; fasten number plates so that they will not swing; be equipped with a muffler or silencer when running; have two lights in front, visible at distance of 300 feet, and one red light in rear, the white lens shining on number plate, making it visible at least 50 feet.

They shall not: display the numbers of more than one state at a time; use any acetylene, electric or other dazzling headlight unless it is shaded; require a New York license, if owner is a resident of and displays the license of another state, for the period of time that such state grants similar privileges to residents of this state.

Driver shall operate the vehicle in a careful manner, so as not to endanger life or limb of any person, and if signaled by driver of draft animal, stop machine until animal has passed. A chauffeur shall display license badge conspicuously on outer clothing when employed.

Operators shall not: if under 18 years, operate a motor vehicle unless accompanied by owner or licensed chauffeur; require a license for the vehicle for 15 days after purchase, provided application has been made for a license and provided a manufacturer's number is being used; drive faster than 15 miles per hour in the city proper, and 25 miles per hour in undeveloped sections; turn corners at more than 4 miles per hour; pass schools on school days between 8 a. m. and 4 p. m. or cross a bridge at a rate of speed exceeding 10 miles per hour; pass or approach within eight feet of a street car which is stopped to take on or let off passengers.

Operators shall not leave the scene of an accident to which they are a party without giving their names and addresses to the person injured, a police or judicial officer, or the nearest police station. (Violation constitutes a felony.)

(Public garages are required to keep a written record of the time of departure and return of every vehicle, the name of driver, owner and license number.)

Private Detectives. Private detectives shall be licensed by the State Comptroller.

They shall not engage in such business for hire or advertise such business unless licensed, or display a license badge unless entitled to do so.

Runners for Steamboats, Hotels and Immigrant Boarding Houses shall be licensed by the Police Commissioner, and display their license card conspicuously.

Sailors' Boarding Houses and Runners. Sailors' boarding houses shall display in a conspicuous place a license issued by the State Board of Licenses, and keep a register of the names of all persons entertained therein.

Runners shall wear a license badge at all times when soliciting patronage.

An arrest may be made or summons served for a violation of the foregoing ordinances governing licenses where the offense is a misdemeanor. Where the violation is a felony, or where the violation concerns minors under 16 years of age, a summary arrest is to be made.

ORDINANCES.

Ordinances are laws passed by the Board of Aldermen, and differ from State laws in that they affect only the City of New York. Violations of such ordinances which may be prosecuted criminally are usually termed *misdemeanors.*

Ordinances are divided into two classes: those punishable civilly by the recovery of a penalty prescribed in the ordinance, and those prosecuted by criminal action in Magistrates' Courts.

Where a fine or imprisonment is prescribed, you must either make summary arrest or serve a summons. Where a penalty is prescribed, note the violation, enter it in your memorandum book, and upon returning to the station house at the expiration of your tour, fill out what is known as a *corporation ordinance blank*. This form will be forwarded through official channels to the Corporation Counsel, who will present the matter to the civil court. Subpœnas will then be served on the offender and the witnesses, and if the accused is found guilty of the violation charged, the penalty prescribed in the ordinance is imposed by the civil court.

Where both civil and criminal punishment is prescribed for an ordinance violation, always prosecute under the criminal section for the reason that quicker action invariably results.

When you observe a corporation ordinance violation, such as merchandise lying on the sidewalk outside of the stoop line, warn the person responsible that it is a violation of the law to have such material on the sidewalk. If he does not remove it promptly, mark the object with a lead pencil, make a note of the time, continue to observe the object for a reasonable time and then serve summons for violation of sanitary code. The usual defense made by persons who are brought to court for this offense is that the articles were in transit, as it is not a violation of law to place goods on the street while they are actually in transit during loading or unloading of a wagon; if you take the precautionary measure of marking the object, you will be able to testify intelligently and truthfully when the case comes up.

The courts have held that no person can erect or permit a permanent obstruction on the street, except something which has been established for the protection of life and property or to facilitate the business of the general public, such as police signal boxes, fire alarm boxes, lamp-posts, drinking fountains, mail-boxes, etc.; and any temporary obstruction on the street, except goods in transit, requires a permit from the proper city department.

A permit of this kind must be in the possession of some person on the ground. You should examine it, note its number, location indicated, date of issue, date of expiration, name of person to whom issued and name of person signing it, and enter these facts in your memorandum book.

Very often it is necessary for a contractor or for gas and electric corporations to open a street for the purpose of making some emergency repairs, and it would be impossible to get a permit to do so from the proper department quickly enough. In such cases satisfy yourself that the work is of an urgent nature, and permit them to continue. Enter in your memorandum book the name of the person in charge of the work, the location, particular portion of the street to be opened, and the reason for same. Your emergency permission is good only until such time as the person doing the work can obtain a permit from the proper department.

Permits.

Principal permits, in addition to those mentioned under "Co-operation with City Departments," are the following:

From City Clerk—To display an electric sign. Sign must be 10 feet in the clear above level of sidewalk and must not project more than 8 feet from building line.

From Board of Aldermen—To drive an advertising wagon through the streets.

From Department of Licenses—To hold religious meetings in street.

Report to Corporation Counsel if necessary permit has not been obtained.

From Police Commissioner—To hold a masquerade ball; for parades and processions in general; and for boarding house runners, stationary engineers and firemen.

Arrest should be made or summons served on persons who have not obtained the required permit.

From City Magistrates or Police Commissioner—Pistol permits. Summary arrest should be made of all persons having pistols without proper permit.

No permits are required for the following:

To place signs or show bills on the front of and parallel to buildings, when not projecting more than one foot, and securely fastened.

To place signs at right angles to buildings when not extending more than 3 feet, and when 8 feet in the clear above level of the sidewalk and not higher than second floor.

To erect and maintain a bridge over sidewalk, if not more than 7 feet high and 6 feet wide, when erecting large buildings.

To have drop awnings without vertical supports within the stoop lines, not extending more than six (6) feet from house line, and when seven (7) feet in clear above sidewalk.

To exhibit goods in front of store, not more than 3 feet from house line and not more than 5 feet in height.

To place show cases and emblematic signs on sidewalks within stoop line, not more than 5 feet high, 3 feet long and 2 feet wide. Must be movable and must not interfere with entrance to adjoining premises.

To place barber poles on sidewalk within stoop line, not more than 8 feet high and not more than 5 feet from house line.

To place skids across sidewalk when loading or unloading merchandise, to load or unload merchandise on sidewalk, or to back a truck on sidewalk for that purpose, when a passageway is left clear for pedestrians.

Violations of Corporation Ordinances.

Violations punishable by fine or imprisonment:

To post, paint, print, or nail any advertisement, poster placard, or sign, upon any flag-stone, lamp-post, tree, telegraph pole, curb, gutter, horse-post, barrel, hydrant, awning post or box in any public street.

To bathe in a public place without being attired in a bathing suit which prevents any indecent exposure of person.

To drive over fire hose in the streets, except with permission of Fire Department. U. S. mail wagons and ambulances excepted.

To throw any fruit or vegetable skin or other slippery substances on sidewalk or crosswalk. Proprietors of places where fruits and vegetables are sold must have a copy of this ordinance posted conspicuously.

To use salt or saltpeter to dissolve snow or ice on sidewalk.

To damage or deface street signs.

To sell or offer for sale, theatre tickets in the street.

To sell or offer for sale, a bean-shooter, or to use one in a public place.

To disturb a lawful meeting.

To trick ride, or carry a child under 5 years of age on a bicycle in a public street.

It is a violation of the Penal Law to place advertising matter upon any real property or structure without the consent of the owner, or place handbills, circulars or cards in letter boxes of tenement or apartment houses unless enclosed in a wrapper and addressed to recipient.

Summons should be served or arrest made for any of the foregoing violations.

Violations punishable by penalty to be reported to Corporation Counsel by means of Corporation Ordinance Complaint:

Failure to: protect areaways with suitable railings;

At night, protect cellar or basement entrance leading from street, with prescribed chains or lights;

Place lights at night on building material or other obstruction in the street.

INDEX

A

B

C

F

I

J

L

M

N

O

P

R

S

T

V

W

www.ingramcontent.com/pod-product-compliance
Lightning Source LLC
LaVergne TN
LVHW010548110826
845149LV00003B/602

* 9 7 8 1 4 1 8 1 8 7 7 2 9 *